Computer Assisted

Language Learning

Computer Assisted Language Learning

Program Structure
and
Principles

Edited

by

Keith Cameron

University of Exeter

intellect books

Blackwell Scientific Publications Ltd
Osney Mead, Oxford OX2 0EL

First published in Great Britain in 1989 by
Intellect Limited
Suite 2, 108/110 London Road, Oxford OX3 9AW

First published in the USA in 1989 by
Ablex Publishing Corporation
355 Chestnut Street
Norwood, New Jersey 07648

Sole Distributors outside North America
Blackwell Scientific Publications Ltd
Osney Mead, Oxford OX2 OEL, England

Consulting editor: Masoud Yazdani
Copy editor: Rowena Gelling
Cover design: Steven Fleming
Acknowledgements: Mrs V Jones, Mrs R Luffman, Miss C Booth and Miss S Moore

British Library Cataloguing in Publication Data

Computer assisted language learning: program structure and principles.
   1. Languages. Teaching. Applications of microcomputer systems
   I. Cameron, Keith, 1939 –
   407'.8

   ISBN 1–871516–01–3

Printed and bound in Great Britain by Billing & Sons Ltd. Worcester

CONTENTS

CHAPTER VIII : Language Tutoring with PROLOG 101

Masoud Yazdani

PREFACE

Keith Cameron

University of Exeter

Recent publications and conferences bear witness to the continuing interest in Computer Assisted Language Learning (CALL). This present collection of essays was born as a result of the second national conference held at the University of Exeter (September 1987). The theme of the conference, *Program Structure and Principles in CALL*, is reflected in the contributions to this book. The collection forms a handbook for the CALL enthusiast, a 'doing' book, designed to assist the researcher and to indicate avenues he can readily explore both in his own research and the elaboration of other people's programs.

As the first four chapters underline, any future work in CALL must be based on practical pedagogical principles. There is obviously a tremendous difference between devising programs which 'should' help people learn and the writing of programs which take into account proven learning techniques and skills.

The aim of developing CALL is not to provide language learners with novelty, (a novelty which in many cases has already disappeared), but is to improve the quality of language teaching. The aim is not to show how ingenious we are in creating software but to use the computer to help us implement educational aims. More use needs to be made by programmers of educational psychology, methodology and linguistic science.

Layout, use of colour, authoring programs, databases, dictionaries, grammars, adaptation of adventure games, etc.; all these things need careful consideration if they are to be utilised profitably.

We have learned how to transfer exercises of the language laboratory type to the computer; we have started to use the computer in an imaginative manner; we now have to continue to explore the various avenues of language learning methods, even if progress must, of necessity, be relatively slow.

One of the points of discussion amongst interested parties is the value of Artificial Intelligence (AI). (See Chapters I, II, VI.) They have raised the question: Is Artificial Intelligence capable of producing an expert system which will reflect all the 'intelligence' a human user of language would possess? Although a program can be designed to include rules of grammar, dictionaries, etc., it is objected that the interpretation of the message is often open to ambiguities which, although solvable by the human user, are not avoidable through programming. It is certain that this is an obstacle in the development of AI, but it seems to me that although the critics of AI are right in absolute terms, we have to consider that communication between humans is not 100% perfect. Ambiguities exist in all our transactions and we avoid them often merely through knowledge based upon experience. It is my belief that if those who research into AI are not too ambitious at the outset, that if the task, in true Cartesian fashion, is divided up into manageable modules, eventually a system which will achieve a high degree of efficiency will result. (See Chapters VII, VIII.) Such a process will take time, but as each new frontier in handling knowledge through AI is crossed, the fruits of the research can be harnessed and developed. As we advance, and as the chapters of this book reveal, there is a need for both traditional CALL and AI techniques to exist side by side, each drawing upon the other's expertise and discoveries. In the same way that we may only become aware of the semantic misuse of a word when it is pointed out to us by other users of the language, it may be expedient to concentrate on a 'thinking' machine which will use the expertise of both the user and a third party by simulating a dialogue situation; the machine making sure that the text is syntactically correct and the third party assuming the responsibility for its semantic correctness.

As we each work with our small or more powerful machines, the problems of memory and storage, of response and turn round speed, become more acute. For the micro user, storage (see chapter V) is of prime concern. For the user with access to a mainframe, constant technological advances will improve retrieval times but s/he should not lose sight of the necessity, even in the early stages of research, of trying to incorporate in her/his program those 'short-cuts' which we all employ in our subconscious use of language. Much can be achieved by exploring the role of probability and analogy in our speech and writing patterns. Exceptions to rules do exist, but, apart from some well-charted common examples, they remain exceptions to a coherent system. We should exploit that system as much as we can.

Another comforting feature of these essays is the obviously practical nature of their orientation. The accent in this volume is on 'teaching', is on the ways in which the computer can be used to enhance learning, without neglecting to indicate precious caveats about doubtful lines of research.

It is hoped that the views put forward in these pages will encourage those who already work in CALL and inspire those who are hesitant to do so. In this way we shall all come closer to what must no longer be an ideal, but a long-term reality, the perfection, or near perfection, of the efficient language teaching machine.

90 0013150 3 TELEPEN

This book is to be returned on
or before the date stamped below

CANCELLED   15/02/94

29. APR 1992

INTER-SITE LOAN
21 NOV 1995
CANCELLED

CANCELLED

14. JUN. 1993

25. NOV. 1993
10. DEC. 1993   28. OCT. 1997
25. MAR. 1994

I

CAN COMPUTERS AID VOCABULARY LEARNING?

Jeremy Fox

University of East Anglia

1. Introduction

This chapter is primarily concerned with the relationship between how vocabulary is learned naturally, and how it is learned in the classroom situation using CAL. There are, however, a number of difficulties with this approach.

The first of these is the comparative lack of theoretical information about vocabulary learning, which has attracted less research effort than syntax. Secondly, language teaching methodologies are frequently not based on properly substantiated theoretical statements. In fact, they tend to be based on assertion, authority and packaging, rather than on research. As Richards puts it:

> Too often, techniques and instructional philosophies are advocated from a philosophical or theoretical stance rather than on the basis of any kind of evidence. Methods are promoted and justified through reference to intuitively appealing assertions and theories, which when repeated by those in positions of authority assume the status of dogma.

Richards goes on to complain about the "subjective and speculative" nature of a famous recent EFL syllabus, which he described as "based largely on the intuitions of its compilers" (1). His criticisms recall those of Sage and Smith's report in which CAL is characterised as "innovation without research". (2)

Apart from the lack of convincing reasearch data to validate choices about methodology, there is another problem to be faced up to from the start. While the

---

(1) Richards, J.C., (1985), *The Context of Language Teaching*, Cambridge, Cambridge University Press.

(2) Sage, M. and Smith, D.J., (1983), *Microcomputers in Education: a Framework for Research*, London, Social Science Research Council.

argument of this chapter (namely that theoretical information contributes towards understanding vocabulary learning and devising viable materials) seems inoffensive and maybe even self-evident, it would be wise not to ascribe too much significance to language learning theory alone. That is to say, methodologies are cultural artefacts, and the product of social and political forces. In specifying a language syllabus, experts may invoke, for example, educational criteria (read the great books, train your mind), political ones (get to know people from other countries) or social ones (pass university entrance examinations). Furthermore, since motivation and attitude are probably the most important determinants of success in second language learning (3), attitudes to foreign cultures are another element in influencing the choice of methodology. Thus, looking at how vocabulary is learned can yield at best only partial insights.

2. Definition of Terms

The terms 'acquisition' and 'learning' are used interchangeably, though 'learning' is preferred since it suggests more effort — acquisition sounds like something that happens to you rather than something you do actively (4). It is perhaps worth noting that even Krashen abandoned using the two terms contrastively in 1982 (5). This is not to say, however, that the distinction between informal language learning (e.g. of the first language, in the home) and formal, classroom language learning is not a useful one.

Vocabulary acquisition is not seen simply as a conditioning process, of learning habitual links between pairs of words. Thus, if one is studying French, to learn that the French for 'cow' is 'vache' constitutes only part of the meaning of 'vache'. The belief that all there is to vocabulary learning is memorising lists of pairs of words 'with the same meaning' dies hard. Translation knowledge will probably be adequate for most comprehension situations, but not for spoken or written production. As Richards points out, 'knowing a word' involves knowing how to use it syntactically, semantically, pragmatically and 'discoursally'.

Naturalistic vocabulary acquisition is often a slow, accretive process. In first language learning, for example, children tend progressively to refine their understanding of new words, sometimes by endlesss interrogation of their parents, or by desperate experimentation ("I don't like a delay. Give me a delay."). For com-

---

(3) Gardner, R.C., (1985), *Social Psychology and Second Language Learning: the Role of Attitudes and Motivation*, London, Edward Arnold.

(4) Terry Phillips: a personal communication.

(5) Miller, G.A. and Gildea, P.M., (1987), "How children learn words", *Scientific American*, Sept. 1987, 86 - 91.

prehension purposes, a 'half-understanding' may be adequate. Second language learners sometimes overestimate the importance of complete understanding of new vocabulary. Thus, Cooper writes of a research project in the Far East :

> In their actual reading, unpractised readers showed excessive veneration for each word, and treated a passage in the English classroom as a quarry for vocabulary. They were not wrong, of course, in regarding a rich vocabulary as vital to successful reading, but they were blinded by words to other vital aspects of reading: for example, the importance of reading and understanding only that which is relevant to reading purposes; and the importance of developing the ability to use the wider context to interpret what one does not know and what one needs to know (6).

Similarly, Hosenfeld advises the L2 reader to 'take chances' precisely by skipping words that s/he sees as unimportant (7). This suggests that the eagerness of some language teachers to ensure that their students 'fully' understand the words in a text (e.g. by administrating pernickety translation tests that accept only one right answer) may be misplaced or even harmful.

In the case of first language learning, it is clear that the vocabulary acquisition of the average child is a remarkable feat (8) This is because it does not simply involve memorising but also classification of words for speedy access. Aitchison mentions organisation of the mental lexicon round:

> initial sounds
> endings
> stress pattern
> stressed vowel
> synonyms (9).

Similarly, Hudson points out how much more complete the mental lexicon is

(6) Cooper, M. "Linguistic competence of practised and unpractised non-native readers of English", in Alderson, J.C. and Urquhart, A.H. (eds), (1984), *Reading in a Foreign Language*, London, Longman.

(7) Alderson, J. C. Urquhart, A.H. (eds), (1984), *Reading in a Foreign Language*, London, Longman.

(8) Miller, G.A. and Gildea, P.M., (1987), "How children learn words", *Scientific American*, Sept. 1987, 86 - 91.

(9) Aitchison, Jean, (1987), *Words in the Mind — an Introduction to the mental lexicon*, Oxford, Blackwell.

than existing printed dictionaries (10).

In building up its own mental lexicon, the child makes use of its knowledge of the world, its deductive powers and its imagination as it works out the meaning of new words (11). Second language vocabulary learning is not identical — for example, the first language already exists as a reference point. Nevertheless, the large part of L2 vocabulary learning that takes place through reading seems to operate in ways similar to that with L1 reading. Indeed, according to Alderson's summary of Ulijn's position, the only difference between first and foreign language readers is precisely in their knowledge of vocabulary (12).

A number of interesting themes emerge from this discussion. In the case of L1 vocabulary learning, the process is protracted, accretive, and laborious, involving deduction, knowledge of the world and explorative intelligence in an active and dynamic process.

In the case of second language vocabulary acquisition, the most common techniques in use, apart from haphazard 'picking-up', are memorising word lists and reading, often with dictionary support. Miller and Gildea (13) have proposed the use of interactive video to supply visual and dictionary-like information to readers at the moment when they need the information; and it seems likely that the use of such computer-based information technology will ease the language learner's task in the future.

3. Some Principles of Vocabulary Acquisition with Computers

It seems clear from the previous section that it is advantageous for vocabulary practice based on CAL to be active and meaning-focused. As Craik and Lockhart (14) suggested, retention is a function of depth of processing, where the depth relates to the meaningfulness and significance of the material to the learner. The more there is active brainwork, the more the learner exerts himself or herself in reaching the answer, the better. This may sound, perhaps, like the conscious and analytical approach to grammar study which has sometimes been decried by acquisitionists. Yet one of the characteristics of the Good Language Learner identified in Naiman *et*

---

(10) Hudson, R., (1984), *Invitation to Linguistics*, London, Martin Robinson.

(11) Aitchison, Jean, (1987) *op.cit.*

(12) Alderson, J.C., (1984), "Reading: a reading problem or a language problem", in Alderson, J.C. and Urquhart, A.H. (eds), (1984), *op.cit.*

(13) Miller, G.A. and Gildea, P.M., (1987), "How children learn words", art.cit.

(14) Craik, F.I.M. and Lockhart, R.S., (1972), "Levels of processing: a framework for memory research", *Journal of Verbal Learning and Verbal Behaviour*, 11, pp.671-684.

al.'s study was the capacity to come to grips with the language as a system (15). So conscious, meaning-focused vocabulary study will have a place in a computer-based system.

Another likely element in CAL vocabulary study is the operation of inference. Problem-solving activities are frequently motivating in themselves, and seem likely to encourage learning. An example is:

single is to married as :
1. rare is to frequent
2. male is to female
3. mango is to fruit
4. give is to receive (16)

To get the answer, the student must first work out the relationship between each pair, frequently by creating mental contexts into which they could fit. This leads to a fair amount of mental linguistic activity.

A third relevant principle relates to motivation. Malone has written on how both computer games and computer educational software can be made intrinsically motivating (17). Among the motivating elements which he identifies are challenge and curiosity. One of the ways in which a CAL exercise can be made more challenging is through giving the learner control over the difficulty level, as in many arcade games. Tuning is also available in some educational material through control of the feedback. For example, in *Storyboard* (arguably the best known, after Cloze, of all the text manipulation programs) the student is offered (in Chris Jones's version) three levels of 'Help':

— getting the first letter of an unidentified word
— getting the whole word
— being allowed to see the whole text

Thus the learner can delicately adjust the difficulty level of the task by rationing

(15) Naiman, N., Fröhlich, M., Stern, H.H. and Todesco, A., (1977), *The Good Language Learner*, Toronto, Ontario Institute for Studies in Education.

(16) Fox, J.D., (1984), "Computer Assisted Vocabulary Learning", *ELT Journal*, 38/1, 27 - 33.

(17) Malone, T., (1981), "Toward a theory of intrinsically motivating instruction", *Cognitive Science*, 4: 333 - 369.

the amount of Help information used. In addition, the learner can choose to do the exercise again.

Curiosity in Malone's work refers both to 'sensory curiosity' (excited by good graphics etc) and 'cognitive curiosity' which seeks 'good form' in knowledge structures, i.e. that they should be complete, consistent and parsimonious. Thus, just as a newspaper reader feels a strong desire to finish a nearly completed crossword, so also a group of students who have done most of a *Storyboard* feel a need to finish it.

The next relevant principle to consider is interactiveness. From the early days of CAL on, a good deal has been made of 'man-machine interaction', and of the instantaneous feedback which a computer can provide. To what degree this automatic responding can rightly be called 'interaction' is doubtful. However, where second language learning is concerned, other forms of interaction are also interesting, such as interpersonal interaction and reader-text interaction. The computer can be very successful in encouraging interpersonal interaction between students as in the case of simulations. The computer sets a task, such as ruling a kingdom. The students take the role of king's advisers and decide how to act. They send one of their number to type in the decision, see what happens, and report back. Here, the computer provides much of the stimulus, but the interacting is between human beings.

Reader-text interaction with computers produces different problems. It is unsatisfactory to expose large amounts of text on the screen, and, anyway, the student needs to develop reading skills of text on paper rather than on screen. In the *Venturereader* suite of reading materials developed at the University of East Anglia by David Clarke and the author, most of the reading materials are given on paper, while the tasks are on the screen. Vocabulary is dealt with both by the availability of a reader's lexicon which gives definitions, collocations, examples in context and semantic fields for identifiably difficult words, and offers the learner opportunities for practice of vocabulary difficulties by games (18). The philosophy of making lexical information available to learners at the time they need it is also developed by Miller and Gildea (19). Since computers are so well suited for speedy information retrieval, it seems possible that lexical databases may become an important aspect of CAL.

A further theme to be discussed is that of the relationship between the task and the wherewithal. The role of tasks in language learning has become particu-

---

(18) Clarke D.F., and Fox, J.D., *Venturereader*. Unpublished suite of CAL EFL reading materials.
(19) Miller, G.A. and Gildea, P.M., (1987), art.cit.

larly important over the last few years both with communicative teaching and with Prabhu's procedural syllabus (20). Few would disagree, presumably, that tasks should be appropriate to the learners' needs, linguistic proficiency and interests, that is that they should be meaningful and relevant. However, it is not enough for the tasks to be well chosen: it is also necessary that the system makes it possible for the learners to fulfil the tasks satisfactorily. This is the doctrine of the wherewithal: don't set a computer exercise without making available the necessary information for the student to do it properly (21).

If this principle is accepted, it becomes necessary to reorganise CAL practice materials, and to incorporate the relevant information. It could, of course, be in book or dictionary form. It is not suggested that this wherewithal information should be presented automatically when a learner makes a mistake, but rather that it should be available if looked for. The sort of information to be contained in a lexical database, for example, could be varied, and include not only the collocations, contexts, semantic fields, etc., described for the UEA *Venturereader* materials, but also concordances such as described by Tim Johns, by which a keyword is displayed in the middle of a number of one-line contexts (22).

Ultimately, one presumes, Artificial Intelligence will come to the rescue and supply intelligent Help systems to deal with students' problems. 'Intelligent' here would mean not simply that the system understood the subject area, but also that it 'knew' about the students (past scores, learning preferences, impatience with machines...), and also knew about how to teach, i.e. how to explain points, organise special practice, etc. However, it seems likely that the contribution of the teacher to language learning is so complex, varied and subtle (and cheap) as to make take-over by Intelligent Tutoring Systems unlikely for the foreseeable future.

Finally, the old principle of active use should be emphasised. If a student comes across a new word, s/he will learn it faster by using it actively. This was another of Naiman and colleagues' distinguishing characteristics of the Good Language Learner (23). It is difficult to implement with CAL practice materials which generally require a prediction of the correct responses. However, interactive techniques like the use of simulations mentioned above offer some possibilities.

(20) Prabhu, N.S., (1987), *Second Language Pedagogy*, Oxford, Oxford University Press.
(21) Fox, J.D., (1986), "Call learning environments and the wherewithal", *UEA Papers in Linguistics*, June 1986, Vols 25 - 26.
(22) Johns, Tim, (1985), "Micro-concord", Mimeo, Dept of English, University of Birmingham.
(23) Naiman, N., Fröhlich, M., Stern, H.H. and Todesco, A., (1977), *op.cit.*

4. Some Implications for CAL Vocabulary Software Design

A number of recent publications discuss vocabulary practice materials for EFL in general, for example those by Gairns and Redman and by Morgan and Rinvolucri (24). Richards gives a more theoretical survey of the field (25). Vocabulary materials specifically for CAL are discussed by the author (26).

Perhaps the first point to underline when discussing software design is its integratability into the overall teaching/learning environment. CAL practice generally forms only part of the total programme, and attempts to base the whole language learning programme on CAL seem as unwise as the completely language laboratory-based courses of the past. The classroom use of CAL needs to be determined by teachers and not by software writers. Only teachers know of the needs and capacities of their learners, and of how best to structure the tempo and variety of the learning experience. Thus it is generally the teachers who should decide how great the CAL element should be in a learning programme, and what role it should play. This has implications for teacher training.

We should not be surprised that students enjoy interacting with other students, and that two learners at a computer may work better than one (though be prone to talk to each other in their L1). Should the computer serve as a presentation or as a 'reinforcement device', for example? Should it be used by individuals, pairs, groups or whole classes? In order to answer these questions it is necessary to think carefully of where in the syllabus to use the computer (if at all). In EFL, text manipulation programs, where the group reconstitutes a degraded text, have proved successful with groups of students, though Windeatt provides some critical comment. He points out how little communicative interaction occurs when students are engaged on a computer-based cloze task (27). He also recommends, incidentally, the use of a greater variety of clues in the materials; the highlighting of certain key sections to provide Help; the accepting of several alternative right answers as in Cloze; and, eventually, the linking to databases and dictionaries. These ideas are similar to those proposed above in discussion of the wherewithal (Section 3, *supra*).

(24) Gairns, R. and Redman, S., (1986), *Working with words — a guide to teaching and learning vocabulary*, Cambridge, Cambridge University Press; Morgan, J. and Rinvolucri, M., (1986), *Vocabulary*, Oxford, Oxford University Press.
(25) Richards, J.C., (1985), *The Context of Language Teaching*, Cambridge, Cambridge University Press.
(26) Fox, J.D., (1984), "Computer Assisted Vocabulary Learning", *ELT Journal*, 38/1, 27 - 33.
(27) Windeatt, S., (1986), "Observing CALL in action", in Leech, G. and Candlin, C.N. (eds), *Computers in English Language Teaching and research*, London, Longman.

Another area of software which has proved popular with students working in Self-Access Centres is tutorial software. This is often fairly low level, 'old fashioned' grammatical or lexical practice of a type sometimes disparagingly referred to as 'Drill and Practice'. Sometimes teachers disapprove of behaviouristic drill, but their students nevertheless remain attached to it. However, if the student has selected the exercise and feels it is helpful to his or her needs, then it should not be dismissed too casually, even if the learning model is not accepted. The same principle is true of verb ending practice with morphologically complex languages like French or Spanish. If the student has selected the exercise and is in control, doing the exercise because s/he feels it will help with tomorrow's test, then motivation is built in and the exercise seems likely to promote learning.

Grading: One interesting clue from first language acquisition studies is that initially learners store vocabulary on the basis of sound, and only later on the basis of meaning (28). One might speculate that early CAL vocabulary practice might emphasise sound and spelling, so that spelling games like the inevitable *Hangman* might be appropriate here. Later on, as meaning becomes more central, word association games, collocation practice, synonyms and antonyms, and Text Manipulation will play a greater role.

Word processing-based activities look particularly promising. Jumbling activities are easily prepared, and require no special CAL software. Many forms of text editing can be carried out with word-processors, which have the added advantage of being authentic and like 'real life'.

The large amount of time needed for vocabulary learning to take place was mentioned in 1.3 above. CAL vocabulary materials can take this into account by providing multiple exposures in varied contexts, so as to give the learner the opportunity to use his or her normal vocabulary learning faculties (guessing, inducing, experimenting, checking, refining hypotheses, etc.) as well as knowledge of the world. Our experience with *Venturereader* (29) suggests that the computer is well suited for setting tasks, and for evaluating certain aspects of them. Increasingly, it seems likely that the computer based systems will improve in offering the learner useful and appropriate information when it is needed.

This Task *plus* Help System *plus* Database approach will surely still need to be designed to fit into a teacher-centred language classroom. If this is done successfully it will offer multiple exposure to relevant language, plenty of productive practice, and useful Help facilities. Furthermore, the various parsers now under development

---

(28) Aitchison, Jean, (1987), *op.cit.*
(29) Clarke, D.F., and Fox, J.D., see *infra.*

can be expected to play a role in these expert Help systems.

The social pay-offs of CAL activity such as vocabulary learning also deserve recognition and exploitation. Communicative language teaching, like *Silent Way*, has demonstrated the satisfaction students can gain from interacting together in tasks they regard as valid, meaningful and entertaining. (Indeed, it may well be in large part precisely the social aspect of communicative language teaching, where students spend much of their time talking to each other, that has led to its popularity with students). (See above). Similarly, group CAL activities like simulations and *Storyboard* and its various clones have proved very successful. Malone's criteria of challenge and curiosity give some clues about the design of materials (30). Student control of the challenge by tuning the difficulty level has been discussed in Section 3 above.

The discussion of the use of word-processors in vocabulary learning introduces another aspect of materials design. This is authenticity, and relates to the closeness to 'real life' activities, and thus 'relevance' of the learning materials. Word-processors are, of course, primarily designed for secretaries working in offices, and are therefore seen, to a certain degree, as part of the world of work. This itself gives them a certain authority, which is perhaps increased through the availability of extra software to help the secretary (and thence the learner) produce perfect copy. This includes such things as spelling checkers, synonym finders, syntax checkers, style checkers etc. Although this software was specifically designed for native speaker users rather than second language learners, its potential is clear. Research is now going on into the use of word-processors to develop second language writing skills (31).

The last theme of CAL software design to be discussed in this chapter is the emancipation of the learner. The idea derives from the humanistic tradition in foreign language learning, and, in particular, from the evaluation of the British National Development Programme in CAL carried out in the late seventies by Kemmis and his colleagues. They write:

> It is possible to conceptualise the activities of students (and of teachers) as 'labour' and therefore to consider how CAL, as a labour-saving device, affects their work. To do this it is helpful to distinguish between authentic labour (valued learning), and inauthentic labour (activities which may be

---

(30) Malone, T., (1981), "Toward a theory of intrinsically motivation instruction", *Cognitive Science*, **4**, 333 - 369.

(31) e.g. Sharples, M., (1985), *Cognition, Computers and Creative Writing*, Chichester, Ellis Horwood.

instrumental to valued learning, but are not valued for their own sake). The justification of some forms of CAL is that it enhances authentic labour, for others that it reduces inauthentic labour. (...)

This fourth paradigm we have called 'emancipatory'. Insofar as it has any coherence, its key concept is the notion of reducing the inauthenticity of student labour. Its curriculum emphasis and educational means are derived from the primary paradigm with which it is associated — for it never appears in isolation except as an impulse to curriculum reform. The role of the computer is calculation, graph-plotting, tabulation or other information handling. Examples of this emancipatory paradigm in CAL include Napier mathematics (where the computer is used to carry out otherwise tedious calculations and where the curriculum reform away from the computer is of a revelatory kind, emphasising mathematical concepts rather that techniques), the Suffolk Local History Classroom project (where the computer tabulates census data for the pupils and where the curricular reform away from the computer is conjectural, emphasising history as hypothesis-testing and the use of evidence), the Imperial College CAL work on fluid flow and heat transfer (a part of the ESP Project, where the computer allows numerical solutions to be found for real-life problems which are analytically intractable, and where the curriculum reform away from the machine is more revelatory, elaborating the notions of fluid flow and heat transfer in more complex and industrially-interesting situations), and some of the CALCHEM work (where the computer reduces the inauthenticity of the learning situation by plotting graphs or carrying out calculations for students as a separate but complementary role to its enhancement of the authenticity of the learning experience in enhanced tutorial CAL). The work of the CALUSG Project in Geography which produces difficult-to-generate quantitative data for classroom use might also be considered emancipatory, but it is as much a saving of labour for the teacher as for the student (32).

To summarise, Kemmis *et al.* are proposing a style of computer use which is oriented not only towards effectiveness but also towards pleasureableness, which reduces the slog of learning, and which is linked to curriculum reform. Although the learner's needs are central, the teacher's needs are also taken into account — the authenticity of her/his labour as well can be heightened with CAL.

In some ways, CAL has achieved this already in language learning. CAL pro-

---

(32) Kemmis, Stephen *et al.*, (1977), *How do students learn?*, Norwich, Centre for Applied Research in Education, U.E.A.

grams can produce tests, ranging from question and answer quizzes to cloze tests. The marks can be tabulated, and their validity checked, by computer programs. Word processors can produce reading or practice material, jumbled or otherwise distorted at the teacher's pleasure. Most importantly, authoring facilities allow teachers to put on to the disk the words or texts that they themselves have chosen as best fitting into a particular stage of their course.

In the future, a number of intriguing possibilities suggest themselves. Tim Johns has already proposed the use of concordances to help learners. Here are five lines from one of his examples with 'at' :

common use. You may probably	*at* this present moment be supported
erial that is not necessary.	*At* this low level of radioactivity
nation have all been employed	*at* one time or another. In the Gove
luoride (UF6), which is a gas	*at* room temperature. Largely becaus
regard to wastes. The wastes	*at* Hanford and Savannah River are m (33)

In each of these lines, taken from a corpus of texts stored on disk, the keyword 'at' occurs in the middle. The concordance provides the language student with authentic data about the behaviour of keywords in genuine language. If the corpus of texts is authentic, then this genuineness is guaranteed. Tim Johns has also proposed the idea of linking a synonym finder (the sort of applications software already available with some word-processing packages) with a concordance program. The student would meet a difficult word, ask for synonyms, and use the concordance program to display examples of any of them in context. This would be one way in which the computer could facilitate the process of vocabulary learning, analogous to the calculation and graph-plotting facilities mentioned above.

5. Conclusion

This rather wide-ranging discussion suggests three main conclusions:

1. It is useful to look at theories of L1 and L2 vocabulary learning for insights into how it should be learned in a CAL context. The varied mental faculties and strategies which are involved, the gradual growth of the mental lexicon and the acceptability of initially partial understanding of word meaning are examples. The stimulus of challenging problem-solving activities, and ones where the learners themselves control the difficulty level, and where their task is to complete incomplete schemata, can increase motivation.

2. Successful vocabulary learning depends upon good teachers. Although students can learn a great deal of vocabulary on their own, particularly by reading, the teacher is in the best position to organise valid CAL practice to lead to vocabulary development. Sophisticated computer-based vocabulary learning systems are not yet in existence.

3. Nevertheless, in the middle to long term, one can foresee the development of powerful intelligent databases in which computer base systems will identify student problems and help students to solve them. It is earnestly to be hoped that they will be recognised as a complement to the teacher's work and not supplanting it; as improving the quality of language education and not of reducing the costs. But will they?

II

SMALL PROGRAMS THAT
'KNOW'
WHAT THEY TEACH

Derrik Ferney

Wolverhampton Polytechnic

1. Introduction

As an introduction to this subject, a few brief comments about the structure which underlines CALL programs currently available would seem appropriate. This is not an easy task, since there are several hundred CALL programs on the market or currently being designed, and the range of *types* of program is also immense. There are dedicated programs, which teach or test particular aspects of language into which new data cannot be inserted, and authoring programs which allow the teacher to insert data testing all kinds of linguistic knowledge. There are single programs and whole suites of programs, the latter aiming to teach a basic grammar of a language. There are programs which make maximum use of graphics facilities as an additional motivating factor for younger learners or beginners in a language and those which are primarily text-based. There are overtly instructional/testing programs and those which adopt a 'learning by doing' approach, incorporating, for example, adventure games (such as *Granville*), simulations (such as airline booking), and even the 'learning by programming' approach described by Papert in *Mindstorms*, where the student learns about syntax and word categories by programming the computer to write phrases.

More recently, much work has been done on linking computers with peripheral audiovisual devices — AECALL/VECALL — to alleviate the computer's deficiencies in the area of the spoken language and to provide additional sources of stimulus. We might also mention here the use of computers as terminals for videotex systems such as the French Teletel service (Harrogate College or Aldoda International can provide the software). Pages from Teletel can be saved to disk and then used locally and cheaply as part of student assignments. Whilst we are on the subject of the computer as a means of obtaining information we might also mention databases which can be used for functions as different as document search and phrase concordance.

Finally, there is considerable range in the ambitiousness of existing CALL programs; the less ambitious, such as vocabulary acquisition programs, might concentrate on single words, possibly in a contextualising sentence; more ambitious programs might deal with the conjugation of verbs or with specific types of phrase which are known to cause problems in second language acquisition. The most ambitious move beyond the phrase to the sentence and to discourse, with tasks such as text reassembly, cloze tests and sentence and supra-sentential translation.

2. Teaching programs

The fact that there are so many different types of CALL programs in existence illustrates the futility of attempting to define a single set of program principles or structures to fit all situations. For this reason, this chapter is limited to a discussion about those programs which are intended to teach students something about grammar, translation or comprehension of a language using primarily a text based approach. There will, therefore, be no direct reference to AECALL, VECALL, adventure games, simulations, databases or learning by programming approaches. First, two observations about the grammar/translation or comprehension programs currently being sold by software houses.

1. Though most of them contain exposition about relevant aspects of grammar or vocabulary, or offer some sort of guidance and help notes, these only constitute an approximation to the type of knowledge a teacher possesses about teaching the subject. A teacher of French, say, uses at least four types of knowledge to do the job — first a knowledge of French, secondly knowledge about teaching and learning, thirdly knowledge about the students taught, and fourthly knowledge about the world. What is more, these types of knowledge have to interact with each other in order to respond dynamically to the behaviour of the student. A computer program which could model all these types of knowledge would approximate to what Masoud Yazdani called the ideal teaching machine at the 1985 Exeter Conference (1). That ideal machine is still a long way off and it is clear that virtually no CALL program currently available seeks to model anything approaching these types of knowledge which teachers possess. It is high time for CALL programmers and designers to address the question of knowledge representation in their programs.

2. The second observation is closely linked to the first one. Nearly all the grammar/translation/comprehension programs currently available rely, for their ability to test students, on a series of questions and answers which have been determined *in*

---

(1) Yazdani, M., (1986), "The ideal teaching machine", *Computers and Modern Language Studies*, Ellis Horwood, Chichester, pp.144 - 153.

advance by the programmer. They rely, in other words, on pre-compiled or 'canned' knowledge about the subject they deal with. The program itself is incapable of either generating or solving the problems it sets the student. Such programs, which constitute the near entirety of current CALL programs, use a structure which pre-stores, pre-compiles or 'cans' a finite set of questions and a linked finite set of acceptable answers to those questions. The program selects a ready-made question, elicits a response, and compares that response with its pre-stored answers. If an exact match is found the answer is pronounced correct; if not, it is deemed wrong and remedial action is undertaken.

Admittedly, more sophisticated techniques can be added to this basic program structure and most of today's programs use them. They include:

1. a variety or hierarchy of pre-stored answers
2. fuzzy matching routines
3. scoring/branching routines
4. recap/review/help routines
5. clue-giving routines
6. error-trapping, which requires the programmer or author to try to foresee the major errors students are likely to make and 'can' them as a set of unacceptable answers with specific error messages attached.

All these techniques increase the flexibility (interactiveness) of the program but none of them compensate for a program structure which can only offer 'canned' solutions to 'canned' problems.

3. 'Canned Knowledge'

Why is 'canned knowledge' inadequate as the sole form of knowledge in a teaching program? Primarily, because it restricts the degree of real interaction with the user. At its worst, and worst is to be stressed, it has been used in highly serial, single question-single answer programs which hark back to the early days of language laboratories and draw their inspiration from programmed learning and behaviourist teaching methods. It is this type of CALL program which drew the fire of leading members of the British Artificial Intelligence 'School' who criticised the 'strictly Skinnerian poverty' of an early vocabulary program which took the form 'What is the German for X?' and, depending on the student's response provided a pat on the back or gave the correct German equivalent, and passed on to the next word (2).

---

(2) O'Shea, T. & Self, J., (1985), *Learning and Teaching with Computers*, Harvester, Brighton.

In making this criticism of what was actually a very early and simple CALL program designed to aid vocabulary acquisition, which any of us might have written, O'Shea and Self revealed the essentially cognitivist outlook of Artificial Intelligence and also betrayed some ignorance of second language learning. With regard to the latter, few language teachers would deny the usefulness of drills in the early stages of language learning and Gagne has adequately illustrated the place of stimulus-response learning in the learning hierarchy (3). Nevertheless, CALL programmers would do well to take on board the spirit of what O'Shea and Self are saying. Many of our programs are based on drill and practice routines, which are of course procedurally simple enough to be ideal candidates for use with micro-computers, but we have to agree with Papert when he says that "paradoxically, the most common use of the computer in education has become force-feeding indigestible material left over from the pre-computer epoch" (4).

We might take the view that it is not the 'canned' data structure *per se* which is to be blamed for producing rather pedestrian computerised drills but rather the lack of *sufficient* 'canned' data, or the pedestrian procedures which manipulate that data. But this is really to miss the point because no matter how much knowledge you attempt to pre-store as 'canned' data your program will still end up constraining students to follow the paths *you* have established through the program. And this clashes with one of the fundamental aspects of learning which is that it is an individual and *creative* process.

Program writers are aware of this and have tried to increase the flexibility of their programs to allow for student creativity by 'canning' multiple solutions to each problem set and by attempting to anticipate errors which the student is likely to make. But this approach — which we might call multi-canning — becomes increasingly time consuming to implement as the ambitiousness of the program increases. Multi-canning, however, can be very effective, as Brian Farrington's well-known LITTRE program (5) illustrates, but the price paid is the sheer slog of working through an English passage with a French native speaker looking for all possible translations of each phrase and sentence. Furthermore, a complex sentence may take several hours to convert into data which can be used by the computer. Once all this work has been done the end product is very impressive — there are numerous possible routes through the program, there are very useful prompts and error messages, and most important the program allows for a great deal of freedom and creativity on the part of the student. The program really does appear to be

(3) Gagne, R., (1977), *The Conditions of Learning*, Holt Rinehart & Winston, London.
(4) Papert, S., (1980), *Mindstorms*, Harvester, Brighton, p.53.
(5) Farrington, B., (1986), *An Expert System for Checking Translation at Sentence Level*, University of East Anglia, Norwich.

knowledgeable about French language, and it holds an important place in CALL research for this reason.

LITTRE also holds an important place in CALL research, however, because it pushes to the limit the possibilities of programs based on 'canned' knowledge, which *it* holds in the form of a variety of good versions of the passage to be translated.

Every prose which is programmed into LITTRE takes, as has been said, many hours of work by human experts to compile, and that expertise, once 'canned' in the form of good translations, cannot be transferred by the machine to another text. You have to start from scratch and repeat the entire procedure for every new prose you want to make available to students.

It would therefore seem profitable for CALL programmers to direct their attention at modelling the *competence* of the human experts as well as simply 'canning' time after time the fruits of that expertise. If such modelling could be achieved, or even partially achieved, then programs would *themselves* be able to generate and solve the very problems they set students.

4. A Knowledge Based Program

Computers can after all be programmed to do much more than match datafiles of 'canned' questions and answers. Let's consider for example what the program structure of a knowledge-based German grammar-translation program might be.

Firstly we would need an expert module which would model the human teacher's expertise with German language or the expertise of a native German speaker. This would comprise a dictionary in which words would be listed along with their grammatical and possibly semantic attributes; it would also contain a model of German phrase structure grammar, or a subset of it. Armed with this knowledge about words and grammar the expert module could generate German phrases or sentences and, conversely, parse student input to check if it is well formed. If it was also equipped with a semantic parser it would be able to check whether the student input made sense. The ability to generate and check phrases or sentences in German opens up the way for considerably freer and more creative exchanges than are possible using 'canned' questions and answers, and the knowledge representation formalisms required to program such an expert module are well documented in AI literature.

Secondly we would need a tutor module. Whereas the expert module would contain rules about language, the tutor module would contain rules about teaching. It would make decisions regarding the selection and ordering of teaching materials to suit what the student module tells it it thinks the student knows or does not know.

The tutor module might contain a variety of strategies for dealing with syntax or semantic errors picked up by the expert module. It might also contain rules telling it when to intervene to correct an error, and when not to intervene, since making errors is a necessary part of learning. In other words the tutor module would seek to model the expertise used by a teacher to modify the approach adopted according to the student's performance in answering the questions set.

Thirdly we would need a student module. This is the area which is most problematic to implement since it is difficult to deduce from a student's observable performance precisely what is going on in his or her head, precisely what conscious reasoning (if any) he or she is using to solve a particular problem. The student model could range considerably in complexity. A simple one might record the number of correct versus incorrect answers, much as current CALL programs do in order to trigger branching routines. It might involve the compilation of a student 'history' or 'profile' which is updated each time the student uses the program, and which contains a record of structures the student is thought to have mastered. It might seek to identify categories of errors. Most ambitiously of all it might seek to assess the student's cognitive style because people learn things in different ways. At present, however, this is beyond the state of the art.

Computer programs possessing a tutor module interacting with expert and student modules would possess a knowledge base with the potential to be far more interactive, flexible and extensible than most CALL programs currently available. They would not run on a BBC-B micro but their power would not derive *solely* from greater computational power. It would derive from the explicit representation within the program of rules modelling the competences of language teachers. Not all of them, perhaps, but even the provision of a part of some of them would be an advance on current CALL programs because, to quote the title of this paper, they would to some extent 'know' what they teach. Furthermore, the time-saving for teachers wanting to use such programs with their students would be enormous.

Once we have succeeded in programming the knowledge required to teach the translation of one text, for example, that same knowledge could be used to teach the translation of other texts of comparable difficulty, provided the dictionary was updated to include new vocabulary. This means that human experts — language teachers and native speakers — would no longer have to spend hundreds of hours canning innumerable good versions of every new prose translation to be presented to their students. The computer would do it for them. In fairness it must be said, though, that the time saved by teachers imparting their expertise must be balanced against the massive investment of time required to write the programs in the first place.

Now all this may appear something of a pipe dream — and perhaps parts of it are. But there are already a number of intelligent tutoring systems in existence. Admittedly they are very large, use vast amounts of computational power, have required man-years of programming and are generally located in the A.I. units of universities and large companies. Furthermore, they tend to be based on expert systems operating in restricted domains such as fault finding in circuitry or the diagnosis of blood disorders. None of them has attempted to come to terms with language teaching, where the number of variables is far higher.

But if we cannot think big yet, we could think small, in the belief that the lessons we learn about knowledge representation and the modelling of teachers and students in *small* programs will be of value as the computers used in education become powerful enough to handle large programs. This *programming principle* should be more widely adopted as it is a strategy which has already borne fruit. There exist a number of small or smallish programs which have succeeded in achieving what we might term 'local' intelligence, i.e. they know just enough, they possess sufficient competence to teach and test particular areas of grammar, syntax, translation or comprehension without resorting to 'canning' (or indeed multi- or even mega-canning). For those who have not come across these programs before and who would be interested to find out more about them, a short bibliography in which they are listed is appended to this chapter. The reports in the bibliography give details of the knowledge representation structures used in the programs and of the results the programs achieve.

5. GENDER MENDER

It might be of interest to consider a modest example of one such 'locally intelligent' program which we have been elaborating. It is the expert module of a system called GENDER MENDER (6) which seeks to model rules about French grammatical gender. GENDER MENDER is not a vocabulary acquisition program as such. It doesn't seek to teach, say, the most frequently used 600 words in the French language, but rather to help advanced learners, who already possess a significant vocabulary, master the apparently arbitrary gender classification system of the nouns they already know.

As the basis of the expert module research into grammatical gender completed by Tucker, Lambert and Rigault was used (7). Their work describes the formulation

(6) Ferney, J.D., (1986), "Design Principles for an Intelligent Computer Aided Language Learning (ICALL) system to teach the Grammatical Gender of French Nouns", *Cognition, Computing & Psychology Report*, Dept. of Psychology, Warwick University.
(7) Tucker, G.R., Lambert, W.E. & Rigault, A.A., (1986), *The French Speaker's skill with Grammatical Gender : An Example of Rule-Governed Behaviour*, Mouton, The Hague.

of a rule system to account for the native speaker's skill with grammatical gender, and the testing of the power and efficiency of that system.

They begin by showing the deficiencies of French grammar manuals in respect of gender determination — deficiencies which stem largely from the fact that traditional grammars, where they give rules about gender at all, do so on the basis of very small corpuses of nouns. In order to obtain a more complete picture, Tucker *et al.* had an inverse dictionary compiled, consisting of all the nouns listed in the *Petit Larousse*, grouped by written endings and separated according to gender. From this they were able to tabulate with a great deal of precision the number of masculine and feminine nouns for each of several hundred suffixes. On the basis of these findings, they were able to predict what gender French speakers would normally assign to nouns, common or uncommon, real or made up, according to their endings. They tested these predictions on native speakers and found that whilst the gender of common nouns is learned to the point where native speakers automatically know the gender, the gender of unknown or made up nouns is worked out using a number of heuristics — rules of thumb. The most important of these heuristics involves the backward processing of nouns from their ending to their beginning until the native speaker can identify the most useful gender predictor, which is the ending of the noun. They then draw on their knowledge of other French nouns with the same suffix, and on their knowledge of rules of gender prediction, to make an educated guess as to the gender of the novel noun. Of course, like all rules of thumb, this heuristic does not always lead to the correct answer since native speakers often over-generalise a given gender predicting rule and are caught out.

What ultimately suggested the computational metaphor for all this was Tucker's observation that:

> Native speakers seem to be efficient information processors who can focus on the ending as the most probable gender marker, and then scan backwards into the word until they can determine in which particular subcontext the terminal phone occurs... The implications of this 'backward processing' phenomenon are tremendously exciting for they suggest that gender classification is an active process which requires a well-developed rule- governed skill dependent upon the speaker's linguistic experience. (8)

This seemed a highly desirable skill for advanced students of French to acquire and a small expert module which would model the most useful parts of it, was

---

(8) *Ibid.*, p.62.

Objectives 5 and 6 are met by allowing part or all of the relevant rule to be displayed.

Now GENDER MENDER's expert is a program of very limited scope but we think it illustrates the type of program principle we should begin directing our attention at. It is a small, knowledge-based program because it contains in executable form the most useful parts of the knowledge possessed by native speakers of French which enables them to work out the gender of nouns. Not all the nouns in the French language of course — only those for which the suffix acts as a powerful predictor, but the aim was never to model the native speaker's competence in total. GENDER MENDER'S expert can predict the gender of about two-thirds of French nouns by its deployment of carefully chosen rules on the one hand and its store of the several hundred exceptions to those rules on the other, and the list of exceptions could be considerably reduced without much visible loss of power by removing the many uncommon and arcane nouns which figure on it.

6. Recapitulation

In recapitulation, the major points made in this paper are as follows :

1. The near totality of CALL programs currently available work by pre-storing or 'canning' a series of problems and solutions. Because such programs store fragments of *performance* rather than model aspects of *competence* they cannot generate or solve problems. Their inability to generate and solve problems means that they cannot respond in any substantial way to creativity on the part of the learner. It also means that they become extremely uneconomical to implement with ambitious and complex tasks like prose-translation.

2. Because of its relative inflexibility and lack of extensibility to more complex problems, 'canning' problems and solutions will not by itself provide an adequate platform for the next generation of CALL programs. We need to concentrate instead on writing programs which contain an internal representation in executable form of the knowledge they seek to impart to the student.

3. This is a realistic task to set ourselves now. Our program *structures* can be based on the type of knowledge representation formalisms already developed by AI research and adapt them to suit small learning environments, following the precedents already established by Weischedel and others. We should, in other words, aim to write small programs which to some extent at least 'know' what they teach. That is the *principle* we should like to advocate, in the firm belief that it is the

prerequisite for significant qualitative progress to be made in CALL (9).

Appendix

Overleaf is a list of suffixes for use with GENDER MENDER, showing their predictive power. Their order reflects their place in the rule base. All figures are approximate.

(9) ICALL Bibliography: Cerri, S. & Breuker, J., (1981), "A Rather Intelligent Language Teacher", in *Studies in Language Learning*, 3, pp.182 - 192; Schuster, E. & Finin, T., (1985), "VP2 The Role of User Modelling in Correcting Errors in Second Language Learning", *Proceedings of the Society for the Study of Artificial Intelligence and the Simulation of Behaviour*, University of Warwick, pp.187 - 195. (Originally published as Technical Report MS - CIS - 84 - 66, University of Pennsylvania, December 1984.); Swann, P., *Computer assisted Grammar of English (CAGE) for Italians*, (1986), CAL Research Group Technical Report No. 58, The Institute of Educational Technology, The Open University; Weischedel, R.M., Voge, W.M. & James, M., (1978), "An Artificial Intelligence Approach to Language Instruction", *Artificial Intelligence*, 10, pp.225 - 240.

PREDOMINANT SUFFIX	*PREDICTIVE GENDER*	*POWER*
A. CONSONANTIC (FREESTANDING)		
1.-ISME	M	(695.0)
2.-OIR	M	(220.0)
3.-AGE	M	(1268.9)
4.-ISTE	M	(512.8)
5.-OME	M	(87.3)
6.-INE	F	(433.15)
7.-ETRE	M	(137.6)
8.-EUR	M	(1482.78)
9.-PHE	M	(72.4)
10.-UDE	F	(40.3)
11.-TE	F	(860.64)
12.-SE	F	(541.44)
13.-AINE	F	(61.6)
14.-ADE	F	(170.19)
		6578.259
B. VOCALIC (FREESTANDING)		
15.-ATION	F	(1169.1)
16.-IE	F	(1736.27)
17.-EE	F	(357.30)
18.-AISON	F	(64.1)
19.-UE	F	(52.1)
20.-ION	F	(627.78)
21.-I	M	( )
22.-O	M	( )
23.-U	M	( )
		4005.138
C. STRUCTURAL		
24.(VOWEL + NCE)	F	(418.4)
25.(SINGLE/DOUBLE VOWEL + SINGLE/DOUBLE CONSONANT)	M	(7836.170)
26.(VOWEL + DOUBLE IDENTICAL CONSONANT + E)	F	(1057.127)
		9311.301
	TOTAL:	*19894.698*

Total number of nouns in the *Petit Larousse* dictionary is 31,619. Therefore, these 26 suffix-rules can predict the gender of over 65% of French nouns with 96.6% accuracy (10).

---

(10) NOTE: These endings cannot yet be implemented, as Tucker *et al.* contains insuffi-
cient data to permit this to be done. They would in any case be better represented
as a structural rule such as,

— IF the suffix is any vowel other than a/e, THEN the noun is probably masculine.

III

DESIGN CONSIDERATIONS IN WRITING CALL SOFTWARE, WITH PARTICULAR REFERENCE TO EXTENDED MATERIALS

David Clarke

University of East Anglia

1. General Background

The following remarks are made in the light of experience derived from the construction of sample sections of a reading skills computer-based programme (1) entitled *Venturereader*, which has been developed at the University of East Anglia (2). Specific examples will be derived from this but remarks on design and methodology are intended to have a wider application.

Venturereader consists of a network of related programs centred on the development of reading skills and vocabulary acquisition. The intention behind the project is to offer a coherent body of material for a learner to work with, providing a sense of integrated, meaningful progress within a single framework, as distinct from the large number of independent computer-based programs commercially available at the present time. Such programs are often used for what is little more than random self-access activity, where the focus of the computer program may or may not have an obvious connection with what is taking place in the main part of the language programme. The *Venturereader* programme aims to provide the learner with an extensive environment of linked reading-based activities, allowing him to explore the whole network in any way which seems most appropriate and interesting. As a result, the learner discovers for himself what the machine has to offer, what kinds of activity are available and can examine the contents of the extensive database. The completed database will contain a large amount of information relating to grammar, vocabulary and discourse. This is not then a system of forcing learners through a succession of hoops, further progress only being allowed after successful performance, and in fact, there is no necessity to attempt all that the computer has

---

(1) 'Programme' is used here to describe the entire network of *Venturereader* 'programs'

(2) Clarke, D.F., (1986), "Computer-assisted Reading: What does the Machine Really Contribute?", *System*, Vol. 14, No. 1, pp.1 - 13.

to offer or to follow any particular path.

Venturereader offers two basic choices of approach, through text or through skills, the skills option consisting of the opportunity to practise further the activities already introduced in the text path as well as the opportunity for the learner to test himself in areas where he might feel he is weak, or indeed in areas where he feels confident. The programme is intended to operate both in the self-access mode and also in the classroom mode, where learners work in small groups with the teacher monitoring progress and providing guidance when necessary. Many of the activities within *Venturereader* are constructed to provide the opportunity for group or pair discussion, thus using the computer as a catalyst to communication in a problem-solving situation. Examples of such activities will be given below during the discussion of other issues. Exploration of the database, on the other hand, as well as further work in the skills and testing areas, would be best performed by the learner working alone.

2. Programming and Publishing

Teachers are not usually programmers and when they do have a certain skill in this area it has frequently been the case that they produce replicas of similar programs already in existence elsewhere. The kind of program which drills grammar or vocabulary is not essentially very complicated but, even so, the teacher would do well to adapt existing program frameworks rather than spending a large amount of time mastering basic BASIC. Thus, on the *Venturereader* project, most of the programming was done with the help of professional programmers who worked to specifications provided by the teachers involved. There were warnings about the difficulty of conveying pedagogical principles to programmers who do not understand the basic principles of language learning, but it was found that by providing sufficiently transparent specifications, a good approximation to what was required could be achieved first time. Little effort was then needed to tidy up the problems that still remained.

Cooperation, we found, between program designer and programmer worked a lot more smoothly than the cooperation between program designer and publisher. For reasons of availability, the BBC-B was used for developing the materials and in order to achieve even a working sample of the *Venturereader* material, two discs were required. Even then, only an extremely small database could be offered and some of the slots in the overall programme remained unfilled. A really effective sample of the materials would take up at least four discs (eight sides) and it soon became apparent that the BBC-B was not the most suitable machine for a project of this kind. While several publishers showed great interest in the materials, apparently appreciating the pedagogical principles which lay behind them, they could not begin to contemplate marketing even a two-disc package, let alone a four-disc one. The necessity for inserting different discs into the drive on instruction from the screen did not seem to be a very appealing one and of course the presence of a double disc-drive cannot be relied upon in all circumstances. Indeed, since even two sides could not be guaranteed on a disc-drive, the optimum format for a commercial, published program would be one side of one, preferably 40-track, disc. The scope became smaller and smaller and it soon became apparent that a project the size of *Venturereader*, which is intended fully to exploit the power of the microcomputer, would have to move to a hard disc system with a vastly increased memory availability. Transfer to a system with more capacity, such as the IBM PC, has not yet occurred. Publication seems remote in the extreme unless the whole package can be reduced to the proportions described above. These facts only slowly emerged as work progressed and clearly substantial funding would be required for the completion of such a project. The remarks offered here are therefore in the context of a goal as yet unrealised but it is hoped that they will be of some interest nonetheless.

3. Orientation within the Programme

A complex system of interlocking programs linked to an extensive database requires a clear means of orientation for the user, who would need to know exactly what he had done already and where he was in the overall system. An extended network of programs has the potential for exacerbating the sense of claustrophobia sometimes experienced by learners using computer materials. The principle of basing the reading skills activities in *Venturereader* on printed texts is one way of reducing the feeling of claustrophobia. The printed text can therefore always be consulted in the course of an activity and reading can be undertaken in the normal way, rather than from a VDU. But even more important to user orientation is the existence of a map of the whole system, both in printed form and in graphics on the screen. Such a map would indicate all the complex branching which will occur in an extended program system and the screen display can graphically represent the movement of the learner through the system and indicate his present position. This will enable the learner to exit rapidly from the current activity and move to another part of the system by the quickest route. Ideally, the required destination could be indicated by a screen pointer, or mouse, to avoid the necessity of moving through a complicated series of menus and sub-menus.

When beginning the programme on each occasion, the learner would log on and the collection of data concerning his use of the material would begin. The initial menu would indicate where the learner left off at the last session and access to the map would show in more detail which areas the learner has already covered. This can be displayed on both the menu and the map in the form of changing colours for sections which have been completed or at least partly attempted and the initial selector bar can load to the position from where the learner might be expected to continue.

While the learner is proceeding with various activities a full record of progress is taken, being loaded into the individual student data file. Some of the information thus stored would be of particular use to the teacher, who might be interested to know which activities were selected and which ignored and, indeed, which were abandoned part way through. A great deal of information can thus be gathered about how learners actually use CALL materials, which kinds of activity they prefer and which areas of the database they use for reference. One of the most powerful uses of the computer in learning is thus its ability to constantly eavesdrop on the learner, even in a self-access situation, and find something out about how learners conduct themselves in a situation where no specific direction of progress is indicated. Learners therefore have to decide on what skills areas they require further work in and it is essential that these choices be recorded. The teacher might then wish to make suggestions on the basis of the recorded data. The personal data would of course be accessible to the learner himself and of greatest interest here would probably be the scores obtained in those activities which involve scoring or testing. At the present time, the data collection facility is only available for some of the programs in *Venturereader*.

As a further orienting device, again essential to avoid claustrophobic effects, there must also be the immediate option of exiting from whatever activity is being undertaken, together with an opportunity to see the solution to the activity being undertaken if desired. This could be achieved by accessing the map and choosing another route to explore or simply by halting the program and accessing the Help option to see part or all of the solution to the current problem.

4. Layout and the Use of Colour

The layout and appearance of an extended system of programs is of course an aspect of orientation. One fact soon became apparent during the construction of the *Venturereader* programme and that was the necessity for consistency of screen design and the use of colour. There is the great temptation to overuse colour and different screen formats, but it was decided to limit the number of formats to the basic modes of presentation – description material for the activities, the activities themselves and pages from the database, would each be identified by a particular layout and combination of colours. The parts of the skills area of the programme which involve testing would also be identified by a particular colour and screen layout. It is advisable, of course, to make the decision concerning the number of different page formats before programming begins because the amount of time consumed in altering colours and layout can be very considerable. As a permanent feature throughout the whole network, there would be a block at the bottom of each screen containing the options of exiting, getting help for the immediate activity, using the map and accessing the database.

Even the colour use just described is not purely cosmetic but part of the orientation procedure, as already indicated. It was decided, however, to extend the pedagogical use of colour to more detailed aspects of the individual programs. Three examples from the *Venturereader* programme are as follows:

(a) Vocabulary tagging for the printed texts. Since practice at informed guessing is part of the vocabulary module, it seemed necessary to indicate to learners those lexical items which were in fact susceptible to guessing. Clearly, the meaning of all words cannot be guessed because of inadequate context while other items are not worth guessing because of their relative unimportance in the given text. A teacher would no doubt convey these facts to a learner and it was felt that the machine should give some indication of the relative importance of different lexical items. Thus when a learner types in a word as one he does not know or is not certain about, that word will appear in green, yellow or red according to its relative importance. Green therefore indicates a high-priority word, both with respect to the present text and also to its transferability. Yellow indicates a word necessary for immediate comprehension, and which is guessable, but which does not have a very high transfer value. Red tells the learner simply that the item selected is either not worth guessing or in fact cannot be guessed.

(b) Colour values for synonyms and near-synonyms. At the stage of the inferencing practice, where the learner is invited to make a guess at the meaning of the word he is unsure about, the section of the text which contains the unknown item appears on the screen. When the learner keys in his guess, it will either be rejected or processed into the text if it is acceptable. The machine is programmed to accept a certain set of words, some of which are close synonyms for the unknown item and some of which are acceptable in the context but cannot be considered synonymous. Close synonyms therefore appear in green while items acceptable with respect to the overall propositional value of the text will appear in yellow. It is clearly very necessary that learners should not leave the program with erroneous impressions about synonymity.

(c) Colour values in *Chameleon*. The *Chameleon* activity, described in detail elsewhere (3) involves the development of awareness concerning the way words derive their meaning from the context in which they are found. A text is presented to the learners on the screen (although a printed version is available) and certain items are highlighted one by one. As the coloured highlight appears, the learner is required to decide whether it seems to be positive, negative or neutral in the context in which it is found. He can change the colour value by pressing the space bar and then recording the choice by pressing Return. Green is used for words which seem to have a positive connotation, red is negative, while yellow is used for those items which appear to be neither. Following feedback, when the computer reveals what it registers as learner errors in the colour values of the words, the same items are presented in new contexts which might suggest the necessity for changing their colour. The learner then makes such necessary changes and feedback on this occasion is immediate.

While there are considerable possibilities in the use of colour for pedagogical purposes in computer programs, it must be remembered that not only might some learners be colourblind but at the present time many monitors are monochrome. Despite these objections it still seemed worthwhile to be very conscious of, and to experiment with, the potentialitity of colour for a pedagogical purpose.

5. Authoring

The *Venturereader* programme as it stands at present is based on a specific set of texts, which are in printed form as part of the complete package. All the activities provided so far relate to these texts in much the same way as a reading skills book will base its activities on the author's choice of texts. Naturally this is a limiting factor but one which can be overcome, at least to some extent, with computer-based materials. There are two possibilities for extending existing programs. The first of these can be achieved by providing instructions concerning how a teacher can alter a program by simple alterations to its listing. The second is to provide a fully developed authoring program which will allow a teacher to adapt the existing program by following screen-based instructions concerning the input of new text or data. These two types of authoring will be illustrated below with examples from the *Venturereader* programme.

(a) *Wordsort* is an activity which occurs in the area of the programme devoted to the exploration of the lexical content of the given texts. In one of the passages entitled 'The Mysteries of the Great Pyramid' there is a considerable number of words related to building and architecture and the *Wordsort* activity in this instance

---

(3) Clarke, D.F., (1986), "Vocabulary acquisition, the computer and the database", *UEA Papers in Applied Linguistics*, Special Issue, pp. 21 - 42.

seeks to extend the learner's awareness of this lexical field. Thus the activity involves sorting a set of 'building' words into boxes labelled with superordinate categories such as 'Military Buildings' or 'Religious Buildings'. When the set of 20 or 25 words has been placed in the different boxes on the screen, feedback then indicates whether certain boxes contain misplaced items. In such a case, the learner returns to the task and, by discussion or dictionary use, seeks to place certain words more appropriately. It is obvious, of course, that not all teachers would wish to work with the lexical items provided and indeed might prefer an entirely different lexical set for their groups of learners. At the present time no readily accessible authoring program is attached to *Wordsort* but it might be of use to describe how it can be altered very simply by a teacher with no programming knowledge.

After the program is running, 'Escape' followed by 'L' can be pressed in order to obtain the listing of the program. It is then a simple matter of retyping two or three lines of data in order to change a superordinate category or indeed the whole lexical set. For example, the data lines:

10000DATAGeneral Buildings, Places of Worship, Residential Buildings, Military Buildings,

10010DATAtemple, 2, fortress, 4, structure, 1, stronghold, 4, mansion, 3, house, 3, church, 2, castle, 4, apartment, 3, erection, 1, chapel, 2, bungalow, 3, cottage, 3, tower, 4, mosque, 2, encampment, 4,

can be changed to:

10000DATABuildings for Entertainment, Places of Worship, Residential Buildings, Military Buildings

10010DATAtemple, 2, theatre, 1, fortress, 4, cinema, 1, stronghold, 4, public house, mansion, 3, etc.

Thus one of the existing superordinate boxes is now labelled 'Buildings for Entertainment' and the items tagged with '1' are allocated to it. Little effort would be required to change all four categories, and the items found within them, to allow a teacher to adapt *Wordsort* to any reading material s/he might be using. Even if a user-friendly authoring package cannot be provided with such programs (although the goal would always to be to make one available), it is straightforward enough to describe simply the means by which the program can be altered in the above way. Indeed, a productive activity can involve the learners themselves providing the items for the database in order to create a further activity for other learners. This again would provide an excellent means of extending a particular lexical area and providing learners with a constructive reason for doing so. It is only when such an authoring possibility is provided that the full potential of computer-based materials can be exploited.

(b) Programs such as *Wordsort* are particularly amenable to the type of authoring just described. An activity such as *Chameleon*, another of the phases in the vocabulary development module of *Venturereader*, would not be so easily susceptible to changes within the listing and would in fact require a prepared authoring package because it involves text processing. In this activity, described briefly in 4(c) above, learners are required to assign a positive (green), negative (red) or neutral (yellow) value to words within the text on the basis of close reading and discussion. Clearly, in order to make this activity sufficiently versatile, the teacher needs to be able to key in her/his own text and colour-tag the words which s/he wishes to focus upon. Thus an authoring package such as that provided with *Clozemaster* or *Storyboard* would be required to process text at this level of complexity.

6. The Limits to Authoring

Ideally, a framework of programs to operate on new texts would be required so that all the *Venturereader* activities could be easily applied to texts chosen by the teacher. The vocabulary module is particularly in need of some kind of automatic processing of lexical data because at present, the materials writers have to comb each text for likely lexical problems and enter them into the database, together with a considerable amount of information about each. For example, whenever the learner keys in a word he cannot understand in the reading text, the program offers him a variety of ways to approach the unknown item:

1. Guess the meaning
2. Examples of the word in context
3. Synonyms and antonyms
4. Semantic field
5. Related difficulties
6. Definition

Clearly the time required to enter data into these six areas for maybe 100 words per text is quite considerable, even if the authoring facility is available. The material for numbers 2, 4 and 6 in the above list could possibly be obtained by having a dictionary on-line, a facility not yet available to ordinary language learners using a computer, but one which is surely highly desirable and one which will become feasible with the wider availability of systems with larger memories. When the learner keys in a particular lexical item, appropriate files will be loaded from the dictionary database and can be accessed easily if the learner chooses to do so. However, in the guessing procedure offered in 1 above, the first step towards making an informed guess is establishing the wordclass of the unknown item. A dictionary database could not provide the wordclass accurately and some kind of parser would need to be attached to the overall package to handle this and other grammatical difficulties which may arise. This is approaching feasibility with programs available at the present time. However, the next stage of the guessing process involves establishing whether the unknown word seems to have a positive, negative or neutral value according to the context in which it is found (an activity related to *Chameleon*). In order to decide these values, only the teacher, at the time of preparing the materials, can make this delicate decision, particularly when the choice is controversial and likely to lead to disagreement among the learners using the program.

Similarly, during the stage at which an actual guess about the meaning is made by the learner (see 4(b) above), it is in fact useful that the machine can deal with both synonyms and non-synonyms which are acceptable in the context, and certainly no text-handling package, however sophisticated, can replace the teacher working with an authoring system to enter the items s/he wishes to be accepted by the machine. Of course, the task of dealing in this fashion with each lexical item in a long text is actually quite impractical and the teacher would in fact have to select certain key items to which to apply this kind of treatment. Theoretically, providing backup material to each lexical item in a reading text might be just the kind of vast task which a computer could be asked to undertake, but until very many more developed artificial intelligence systems are available, based on an enormous corpus of language material, there will be no alternative to selective authoring by the teacher. Both time and the ability to perform the task of authoring militate against complex authoring.

The question of feedback to learners as they progress through an activity also raises complications in the area of authoring. The more sophisticated the feedback provided by a program, the more difficult it will be to apply authoring facilities to it. An example of a program within *Venturereader* which seeks to offer a fairly high level of guidance to the learner is entitled *Shift*. In this activity learners attempt to place extracts from a text into their proper positions. The text itself is printed out, but separate paragraphs from it can be called onto the screen and the extracts can be inserted wherever the learner feels appropriate. Having placed the extract into the paragraph, confirmation of its position can then be obtained. In order to avoid the simple 'Yes, you're right...Wrong, try again' type of unhelpful response, the program attempts to simulate what a teacher would in fact do in such a situation.

A teacher would not simply say 'Try again' in the case of a wrong attempt, nor would s/he give the answer. S/He would in fact provide some kind of lexical or semantic guidance in order to improve the quality of the second attempt. *Shift* in fact provides several levels of feedback. If the wrong paragraph is chosen for the insertion of the extract, a generalised lexical or semantic clue is given to send the learner back to the text in order to identify certain features there which will help with the placing. If the wrong paragraph is chosen a second time, a more detailed and more direct suggestion is given and only on the third wrong attempt is the correct paragraph indicated. Similarly, if the wrong position in the correct paragraph is chosen, then a clue based on available discourse markers is provided.

While it is relatively simple to provide an authoring package to handle a new text and new extracts, with spaces provided for the specific clues, it would clearly require a fairly proficient teacher to be able to provide effective clues for each wrong step in the activity. At this level, the teacher is being required not simply to author an existing computer program but to become a materials writer to some extent. All teachers would not be capable of performing this task and many would not have the time even if they were able to. The limits of authoring are then reached and the really attractive features of a good computer program — the semblance of artificial intelligence at work, providing individual guidance — cannot really be achieved at the level of programming which is available at the present time.

7. *Conclusion*

While the present discussion has not described a finished product, it has attempted to indicate some of the considerations and problems involved in writing extended software for microcomputers. Despite the difficulties indicated, it seems imperative that a more vigorous move should be made in a direction away from 'single-activity' software, which is not integrated within a teaching programme and which leaves learners with a feeling of not quite knowing why they have been engaged with a particular program. Too little is at present known about what users do in fact learn from using the many and attractive stand-alone programs now available. To an extent, they may provide a valid environment for language acquisition, often being entertaining to the point of addiction. But they hardly make use of the computer's great potential for providing a much larger and self-contained environment conducive to both acquisition and learning, involving many integrated activities and a large database. While some of the impediments to achieving such a goal have been recognised above, any software which does not attempt to exploit fully the power of the machine in this way might reasonably be seen as essentially trivial.

IV

DESIGNER LABYRINTHS
TEXT MAZES FOR LANGUAGE LEARNERS

Osman Durrani

University of Durham

1. The Didactic Text Maze

Like the garden maze, the literary labyrinth has a long and intricate history; some authorities would go so far as to maintain that the concept of the labyrinth is fundamental to western art and literature (1). It comes as no surprise, then, to find that teachers have for some time been experimenting with didactic materials which have been constructed along the same basic principle. In these, the learner, instead of merely absorbing facts, is repeatedly placed within a challenging situation that demands an immediate response. An entire manual may be composed of passages of descriptive text, each section of which is followed by an instruction to select one of several choices which are displayed at the foot of the page. Examples of teaching material conforming to this pattern include A. A. Zoll's *Dynamic Management Education* and Berer and Rinvolucri's English primer *Mazes. A problem solving reader.* In these textbooks, as in certain 'fantasy gamebooks' of the *Forest of Doom* and *Starship Traveller* variety, the reader does not proceed linearly from the first page to the end, but faces choices at the end of each paragraph or section of the narrative. Here the text 'branches', and each reader must make an individual decision, based on the information conveyed in the preceding text. A typical passage from *Mazes* reads as follows:

> PARKING You have left a note on your neighbour's windscreen, asking him not to block the entry to your driveway. He tears up the note, puts it carefully in an envelope and puts it through your letter box.

> What do you do now?

---

(1) The most thorough investigations of this question are provided by Hocke, Gustav René, (1987), *Die Welt als Labyrinth. Manierismus in der europäischen Kunst und Literatur*, Rowohlt, Reinbek (originally published in 2 volumes, 1957 and 1959); and Koerner, Joseph Leo, (1983), *Die Suche nach dem Labyrinth*, Suhrkamp, Frankfurt.

5 Go up to him and ask him not to block your driveway.
14 Let his tyres down.
12 Decide to do nothing, so you have to park in the next street as there is
no room in your street. (2)

Having contemplated the various indicated options, the user must now decide
which is likely to be the most efficacious one in the circumstances. Skipping any
intervening text, we may choose to proceed directly to section 5, 14, or 12, where
new instructions and a further set of options will be displayed. Eventually, an 'exit'
from the maze is reached, although, as in the garden maze, it is not necessarily where
one would initially have expected it to be. The objective, in either case, is the same:
to devise the most direct and effective method of emerging from the exercise. In
order to do so, it may be necessary to retrace one's steps, or to go through the same
section several times, experimenting with several alternative routes.

The very notion of a 'maze' has connotations which are both benign and men-
acing. Reflecting on the meaning of the word in the abstract, it can be difficult to
decide whether to treat it as an elementary pastime for the young or as a sophisticated instrument of torture; but since it has now made its debut as a teaching tool,
it behoves the profession to debate its merits and its faults, and to see how it can
be adapted to the needs of the language learner. I intend to give a short account
of the history of the computerized 'text adventure', and then to examine examples
of some of the most widely used derivations available to the language teacher in
Britain today. This being a relatively new and still largely untested medium, it
must be acknowledged that the exercises to be discussed will not, by themselves,
solve the age-old problem of how to make the teaching of foreign tongues relevant
to the needs and experiences of the student. It seems highly probable, though, that
these methods will lead to further ideas on program design, and eventually serve
as stepping stones to the more comprehensive and integrated CALL courses of the
future. I intend to concentrate on the following commercial programs: *Granville,
the Prize Holiday Package*, (1986), Cambridge Micro Software (= GRANVILLE);
Incendie à l'hôtel, (1985), Wida Software (= INCENDIE); *Manoir des Oiseaux*,
(1986), Camsoft (= MANOIR DES OISEAUX); *Schloss Schattenburg*, (1986), Camsoft (= SCHATTENBURG); *London Adventure*, (1986), Cambridge ELT Software
(= LONDON ADVENTURE); *Por Favor*, currently under development at Ealing
College of Higher Education (= POR FAVOR). All of these were originally designed
to run on the BBC micro, but more recently, several of them have been or are being

(2) Berer, Marge and Rinvolucri, Mario, (1981), *Mazes: A problem-solving reader*, Heine-
    mann, London, p. 18.

modified for use on larger, networked installations such as those based on the IBM PC, and/or are in the process of being rewritten for use in teaching other modern European languages. Inquiries to the above-mentioned publishers should yield up-to-date information as regards the current implementation of these and other CALL programs of this type.

2. The Computerized Text Adventure

The computerized 'text adventure' offers several distinct advantages which no other form of text labyrinth can provide. As with many other types of computer-aided exercise, there is an in-built facility to calculate a score which provides the user with a useful indication of how the session is progressing. This score would typically be based on energy points (SCHATTENBURG, INCENDIE). It might also prove desirable to set a time limit within which certain actions have to be carried out (LONDON ADVENTURE, SCHATTENBURG). Other features designed to pace the learner could be accommodated within the program, for example, a routine providing access to beginner's or advanced levels of the exercise, which might be made dependent on the user's rate of progress.

The main strength of computer-aided adventures resides in the fact that, in such exercises, no-one can take short-cuts or cheat by examining the consequences of the options they face before deciding which one to choose. On the machine, only one option can be pursued at any time, and once a choice has been made, it becomes difficult — if not impossible — to examine what might have happened had the user selected a different route through the labyrinth. The only means of testing alternatives may be to re-start the program. Each move therefore requires careful attention — much more so than when turning the pages of a book. It calls for a coherent overall strategy and involves risks. Perhaps this is what accounts for the popularity of the original computerized text labyrinth by William Crowther and Donald Woods. It was written in FORTRAN, a language not exactly noted for its string-handling capabilities, and was implemented on the DEC PDP- 10. It required some 300 kilobytes of memory, so that in the early days the only computers capable of running *Adventure*, as it was known, were located in large companies and in university science departments; in fact many engineers and physicists still blush at the recollection of how they used to take time off from their research to go boldly into the underworld and ponder the uses of a platinum pyramid in that imaginary world of meandering subterranean passages where untold treasures were hidden. Eventually, it reached wider audiences when it was converted for use on the Commodore Pet by Jim Butterfield. The program is still available today, though subsequent versions have been re-christened *Colossal Adventure* or *Colossal Caves*. A recent survey in the United States has shown that when a company installed the program on its in-house computer, an average of two weeks' work was lost through staff experimenting with new strategies during office hours (3). It was quickly recognized that a new addiction had been born, and, as with most addictions, it was to prove highly lucrative to harness the object of the addiction, devise an eye-catching package, and make it commercially available to as large a number of addicts as could be found, or rather, created.

Soon a number of programmers were trying to improve on the *Colossal Caves* recipe. One of the first to do so was Scott Adams, who came from an academic background at the Florida Institute of Technology. He wrote *Adventureland* in 1978, which reached large audiences on the Radio Shack TRS-80, and was compiled into a mere 16 kilobytes of machine language and thus much faster than anything that had preceded it. It also featured a split screen, with objects and locations shown at the top, and the 'dialogue' between the player and the program at the bottom. Further improvements that have been introduced include the provision of high-resolution graphics (*The Hobbit*, *Valhalla*, *The Pawn*), and a parser that can cope with natural language (4). In most of today's adventures, you are no longer restricted to commands of the 'go north, take rod, light lamp' type, but can reasonably expect the computer to understand more complicated clauses, such as 'Drop all the books except the black one' (*Zork*).

Now it must be admitted that titles like *Zork* sound horribly down-market, and most EFL teachers are likely to have certain well-founded reservations about teaching English with the assistance of a package entitled *Dungeon Adventure* or, worse still, *The Leather Goddesses of Phobos*. Do such programs have anything to commend themselves to the pedagogic profession other than their proven addictive-ness? Are they, in the end, little more than text-based versions of the space-invader breed of zapping games which demand no more than good reflexes?

It is not difficult to appreciate that even the crudest electronic text adventure is an infinitely superior specimen when compared to the arcade game. In its orig-inal form, it makes no use of sprites, sound effects, or that lethal instrument of doom, the quick-firing joystick. Its only medium is the text on the screen, and the response it requires from the user must necessarily be a thoughtful and considered one. To which one could add that the current craze for this pastime owes not a little to the research and methods of the teaching profession. The pedigree of the computer-based adventure is impeccable, including among its principal forebears the

(3) Gerrard, Peter, (1984), *Exploring Adventures on the Spectrum 48k*, Duckworth, Lon-don, p. 8.
(4) Campbell, Keith, (1983), *The Computer and Video Games Book of Adventure*, Mel-bourne House, Tring, pp. 9-11.

sometime Merton Professor of English at Oxford, and the Massachusetts Institute of Technology. Professor Tolkien did more than anybody to get people interested in the potential of the intelligent fantasy novel, and it is a short step from *The Lord of the Rings* and *The Hobbit* to those enormously popular role-playing fantasies of the 'Dungeons and Dragons' variety that now turn up disguised as books, T.V. programs, board games and computer software. At the same time as these were appearing on the market, the M.I.T. was conducting research into computational linguistics and artificial intelligence. Their work included the analysis of natural language by computer, and the development of increasingly powerful parsers. As we know, their findings are paying off in areas as far apart as robotics and medical diagnosis. Problem-solving by computer became a major growth area for scientific research, and the invention of puzzles receptive to computational analysis was and is a priority in artificial intelligence research. One technique to be developed with this end in mind was the creation of finite 'microworlds' equipped with a limited number of locations and objects which required analysis and manipulation. In the computerized text adventure, this approach combines with the time-honoured practice of using simulations to teach life skills. This has a long history, as there are many situations in which it is just not practicable to learn something by doing it for real. For obvious reasons, it is much more convenient to teach first aid, social work practice, investment strategy and navigation by simulation.

The structure of the adventure program can be represented in various ways. We can visualize it as a sequence of problems, in which each correct solution is rewarded by more information, a new problem to solve, and by the addition of one or several points to a score total. An error may have the effect of reducing the accumulated score, as might the lapse of time. Another method to visualize it would be to use a tree diagram, as Berer and Rinvolucri do (p.6), but this creates the misleading impression that the various 'branches' trail off in different directions, whereas in practice most of them eventually link up with some of the others. Therefore the most common way of showing the structure of this type of program is by a series of lines linking boxes which together make up a maze. Since the maze is never depicted visually but only implied by the text printed to the screen, these programs are properly referred to as 'text mazes'. The user, working through the program, may find it helpful to take notes and will probably try to draw a plan of the locations visited; the precise shape of the maze has to be deduced from whatever textual information is shown on the screen.

One of the greatest benefits of the on-screen text adventure is that, provided the user can respond to the scenario that the programmer has created, it is possible for the learner to forget the classroom, the teacher, the 'learning process' altogether, and to pick up vocabulary and idioms of the foreign language almost sub-liminally, while engaged in some other, intellectually no less demanding task. A well-constructed teaching program will convey much besides; for example, GRANVILLE and POR FAVOR should equip anyone who has never been to France or Spain with a good knowledge of the value of the French and Spanish currencies, the use of local transport facilities, the wording of unfamiliar-looking menus in restaurants, and other thoroughly practical matters. The method of instruction strives to imitate the way small children learn their own language. Linguistic exercises of the drill-and-pattern variety are deliberately ignored, while attempts are made to hold the learner's interest by plunging her/him into a situation requiring intelligent responses. One of the first adventures written for language learners was FRENCH ON THE RUN by Gabriel Jacobs, in which the student had been shot down behind enemy lines during World War II (5). Within the terms of the program, correct responses suddenly became a matter of life and death. In another such program, INCENDIE, the linguist must escape from a burning building.

3. Classroom Applications

What are the main advantages of the text maze when compared with other types of program design that have been implemented for CALL exercises? In maintaining the learner's interest, the branching structure of the maze is without doubt inherently more stimulating than the linear or circular structures of routine exercises of the drill-and-pattern variety. Constantly faced with fresh choices, the user becomes aware of having a large measure of control over the run-time execution of the program, and is not made to feel the passive victim of an unrelenting, and in some cases unstoppable, machine. The pioneer spirit is easily kindled by such exercises, as the student experiments with different strategies. Ideally, a small group of students would share a terminal and discuss the next steps amongst themselves, preferably using the target language for communication. Interesting simulations have been produced for the amateur historian: DRAKE and '1914' permit the computer user to take decisions that either Sir Francis Drake or the generals of 1914 might have confronted, and then observe the consequences. An invitation to 'rewrite Shakespeare and survive' was recently issued to would-be emulators of Macbeth (6). For the language learner, this type of activity provides an ulterior purpose to the linguistic exercises; a series of small tasks must be performed in the correct order, so as to achieve a stated objective. As the task becomes more demanding, the importance of correctly understanding the text is increased. In GRANVILLE, there

---

(5) *FRENCH ON THE RUN* is marketed by Database publications, Stockport, Cheshire.

(6) Higgins, John and Johns, Tim, (1984), *Computers and Language Learning*, Collins, London, p. 66. DRAKE is available from LCL, Staines; *1914* is published by Cambridge Micro Software.

is no direct threat; all you have to do is survive for 5 days in a French seaside resort without dying of starvation or running out of money. The operating system issues timely warnings if you are likely to do either of these. But in many of the available text mazes, the scenario is considerably less friendly than in GRANVILLE, and the risks that must be faced are often dire. INCENDIE has you waking up in a smoke-filled hotel bedroom, and if you can't make it to the ground floor in 160 moves, you stand to be roasted alive. In MANOIR DES OISEAUX you are a detective charged with solving a robbery in the highly disreputable country mansion of the same name. One of the residents' possessions has been stolen, and the only way of exposing the culprit is by interrogating each of the 14 guests in turn. They are all endowed with insalubrious personalities, and appear equally untrustworthy. None of them suspects the real criminal. The truth will only be uncovered by a laborious process of elimination: all statements must be collated, and eventually a contradiction in the evidence will reveal the guilty party. Randomization of the 25 rooms, 14 residents and 12 precious objects ensures a prodigious variety of situations.

SCHATTENBURG is a castle located in a remote and mysterious landscape. After coping with a succession of hazards (dragons and other wild animals, deep ravines and tortuous underground passages), the user must identify a concealed entrance to the castle, and then track down and dispose of its tyrannical occupant. In this adventure, no text need be typed in by the student; all available routes are shown on screen and a numerical option is all that is required; the emphasis is on comprehension and analysis. As in INCENDIE and MANOIR DES OISEAUX, there is a clearly defined purpose on which the learner is expected to focus. Each successive piece of information shown on the screen must be incorporated into the user's overall strategy. Correct understanding of the foreign text is vital to success, and it is hoped that students will respond more readily to this form of directed vocabulary acquisition than to texts presented to them for no ulterior purpose.

The labyrinth is both a simplification of, and an elaboration upon, the real world. The geometrical patterns of the mazes at Hampton Court or Hatfield House are stylised miniature reproductions of pathways and tracks in a garden or forest. In the electronic teaching package, these labyrinthine patterns can be represented by the straight lines and loops of the flowchart. Paradoxically, while simplifying, the maze also diversifies, stretching a fundamentally simple pattern by making it increasingly elaborate, lengthening the distance between two adjacent points to an extraordinary degree. It could, therefore, be presented as the ideal teaching tool, in that while interesting and motivating the learner, it simplifies the subject and also provides scope for the consolidation of learning through repetition. The real world is ever present as the basis of the program, especially in simulations such as

GRANVILLE and POR FAVOR, which feature locations in the towns of Granville and Cáceres respectively. An element of fantasy, however, is a useful adjunct. True, any language student might wake up in a burning hotel. Anybody who has spent a night on the Route national 20 and watched the gas-filled tankers rumble down country lanes to avoid paying the French motorway tolls will appreciate that the scenario used in INCENDIE could all too easily become a frightening reality. As for the characters encountered in MANOIR DES OISEAUX and SCHATTENBURG, the student is no more likely to believe in them than in characters from fiction. The strength of such programs lies in their ability to present a striking situation within a strictly limited framework (the 'microworld' of the computer simulation), and to convey a controlled vocabulary and syntax, while obliging the learner to use his or her imaginative powers in a more or less fantastic problem-solving role.

There are numerous beneficial spin-offs from the basic 'adventure' situation. POR FAVOR, GRANVILLE, and LONDON ADVENTURE provide maps of real places and lessons in topography as well as in spoken Spanish, French or English. LONDON ADVENTURE produces a simplified Underground map on the screen, thus acquainting the EFL student with that real-life maze which any visitor to the capital must learn to negotiate. GRANVILLE conveys a great mass of information about a typical French seaside town. There are many supplementary exercises that can be set in this environment. A number of examples are given in the worksheets starting on p. 45 of the accompanying handbook. They range from simple questions about matters of vocabulary to complicated tasks like working out the system of fares used on the Granville buses. The authors of LONDON ADVENTURE also envisage the program being used as a basis for tactical problems such as working out the quickest routes from one place to another. Moreover:

> A number of oral activities could be undertaken as follow-up work. Di-
> alogues could be written and short scenes acted out in pairs using the
> language encountered in the program. Using a map of central London,
> students might be given a number of specific locations from which they
> must get to a bank. The dialogues could give a number of alternative
> routes to the bank, in response to appropriate questions. Students could
> also be encouraged to imagine the sorts of linguistic problems they might
> face if, for example, [...] they cannot find the items they want to purchase.
> *LONDON ADVENTURE Handbook*, p. 5.

All this provides scope for discussions in class; there is, in fact, a welcome tendency in recent programs to encourage students to move away from the monitor and discuss the program (and maybe not just its better points!) in the classroom. Higgins and Johns stress the importance of the 'briefing- execution-debriefing' process when working with computer-based exercises (7). Post-mortems of this type are facilitated by the printout routines which some of the packages include and which provide material for a variety of communication exercises. In GRANVILLE, for example, a diary is automatically compiled as the student moves from one activity to another. This generates useful hard-copy for future reference. The diary is also stored on the program disk, thereby permitting the curious teacher a peek at the records, in order, perhaps, to discover which pupils have been buying cigarettes or spending all day at the gaming tables of the casino. SCHATTENBURG also includes a printout option (Commodore and IBM versions only), which reproduces the text of the adventure and may help the student with the extensive vocabulary (some 2,000 words in total) of this complex program. Hard copy of the text also encourages the student to develop new strategies for use on some future occasion. The printout of the SCHATTENBURG adventure can run to ten sides of A4, or more if a circuitous route is chosen, and this in itself constitutes a miniature textbook which the learner can peruse at leisure.

One complaint that is sometimes heard about this type of program concerns the relative inflexibility of the material. Many programs run the risk of appearing either too complicated or, conversely, become repetitive after only a few minutes. Roger Woodward, the author of MANOIR DES OISEAUX, has come up with an appropriate solution, allowing his program to be altered without too much difficulty, and has provided a veritable programmer's manual in the accompanying instruction booklet. Many of these programs, including SCHATTENBURG, can be altered in this manner, although some are too heavily protected to permit any tampering by the uninitiated. A thorough testing of the programs mentioned above ought, nevertheless, to enable anyone with some programming knowledge to adapt the fundamental design of the labyrinth to their own teaching needs. There are also many manuals dealing with the specific problems raised by this type of algorithm, and some authoring packages have been marketed to take the sweat out of drafting all those clever little subroutines (8).

Finally, it is worth drawing attention to that other forte of computer simulation, the introduction of random variations. When a book is printed, its text is struck into stability and becomes immutable. Not so the computer program. It is possible to devise a routine capable of generating mazes that will be different in size, shape and contents each time the computer is powered up. In practice, there is little scope for generative routines within text adventures. Even experienced

---

(7) Higgins and Johns, *op. cit.*, p. 67.
(8) One such authoring system is *The Quill*, (1984), by Graeme Yeandle, Gilsoft.

adventurers appreciate an element of familiarity, not least because most problems cannot be solved at the first attempt. If you abandon your quest half-way through, or save your position at the end of an hour, it would be frustrating to find yourself transported to a totally different microworld the next time round. There are a great many mazes in which no changes of any kind occur. Thus there are no major variations in GRANVILLE or INCENDIE. Since the user has to accomplish a great many tasks in these programs, this does not matter very much, though I feel that GRANVILLE could have been made more interesting by the addition of a few surprise questions in the 'Quiz' sections. But many of the programs would be of limited use without this variety, just as a maze with half a dozen passages would not represent a real challenge. MANOIR DES OISEAUX solves this problem efficiently by leaving the overall design of the maze constant, but changing the functions of the rooms and the whereabouts of the characters and the stolen goods. In SCHATTENBURG, a number of random features ensure that no-one can solve the mystery simply by remembering a set sequence of key-presses. Some routes are liable to be temporarily closed or otherwise inaccessible. A password is needed, which will be different each time the journey is undertaken. Also, the order in which the most common options, especially 'North/south/east/west', is presented on screen, is always scrambled, thus ensuring that the text is carefully re-read before a key is pressed. The best programs are probably those which harness the computer's ability to produce variations, without over-using such innovative features in a manner likely to confuse the student.

Over the centuries, labyrinths have been constructed from wood, stone, sand, and turf; their passages have been separated by walls, planks, yew trees and privet. They have been found in Crete and Egypt, Greece and Rome, in Gothic cathedrals as well as in the grounds of secular mansions; they serve the most disparate purposes, ritual and recreational, secular and religious, instructive and punitive. As we have seen, the 'problem-solving' maze has been gaining in popularity as an improvement on the text in which everything is predetermined. It is thus fitting that the teaching profession should be turning towards the use of computer-generated model labyrinths not to frustrate or confuse, but to lead students on towards a better understanding of language with the help of tasks requiring an open mind, logical thought and perseverance. The added bonus is that they may learn a little more about life in the process:

What is this mighty labyrinth — the earth,
But a wild maze the moment of our birth?
Still as we life pursue the maze extends,
Nor find we where each winding purlieu ends;

Crooked and vague each step of life we tread,
Unseen the danger, we escape the dread... (9).

---

(9) 'Reflections on Walking in the Maze at Hampton Court' (*Anon.*, 1747); see Matthews, W H, (1922), *Mazes and Labyrinths*, Longmans, Green and Co., London, p. 199.

V

ASPECTS OF TEXT STORAGE
AND
TEXT COMPRESSION IN CALL.

Laurence Wright

U.C.N.W., Bangor

1. Introduction

What is the relevance of improved text storage and of text compression for CALL programs? There are two main potential advantages: saving space (or rather getting more text into the available space) and (possibly but not necessarily) reducing the time it takes to perform some operations. Are these things important? Possibly not, if the computer is big and fast, or the program in question does not involve large amounts of text, and does not have any 'bottlenecks' where slowness is apparent. There are, however, two reasons why they will often be useful in language teaching programs. Firstly, many language teachers will still be using microcomputers with limited memory, such as the BBC B, many years from now. Secondly, there will be an increasing demand for programs which cope with some of the complexities of language. We all of us know that the answer to the question "How do you say such-and-such in French?" is not always simple, and the more complicated the answer becomes, the more text there is to store.

This chapter is concerned principally with small microcomputers, and concentrates on those aspects which seem most relevant to the writing of language learning programs.

2. Text Storage in BASIC

Causes of Wastage: BASIC, the language most commonly used for CALL programs, is convenient for many reasons, but is less than 50% efficient in its use of space for storing text for two main reasons: the way in which strings (whether on their own or in arrays) are created, and the way in which space is allotted to these strings.

The biggest loss of space occurs because the text of strings is usually stored in duplicate. By the very nature of BASIC, text must be presented to the BASIC interpreter during the course of the program for it to be copied into strings and string arrays. This means that whether this is done by declaring the strings (e.g. line$="line of text") or by reading them from a DATA statement (e.g. READ line$(J%)), the text will occur both in the program itself and in the variables which it creates. There are various ways round the problem. We will briefly outline three of them, all involving input from disc.

Disc Overlays: In this well-known technique, the program is divided into a main body and various segments, each of which is loaded from disc to over-write the segment previously loaded. The commands to load the overlays must, of course, come from the main body of the program, as follows:

> Load main program
> Raise LOMEM (the start of space for variables)
> Dimension the string arrays, etc.
> REPEAT
> Load an overlay at TOP-2
> Use it to put text into the string arrays
> UNTIL all the text is in the string arrays
> Load another overlay at TOP-2
> Continue with the program

> *Example 1a*: Using disc overlays

The line numbers of the overlays must be higher than those of the main program.

Inputting Text from Disc: Instead of reading text into strings from DATA statements, they can be read from a disc file, using the INPUT# or BGET# statements:

> Open a disc file for input
> REPEAT
> Read a string from disc into a string variable
> UNTIL the file is ended or all string variables are filled.
> Close the file
> Continue with the program

> *Example 1b*: Inputting text strings from disc

One advantage of this method is that the strings can be written on a word-processor such as View or Wordwise. The main drawback is its slowness, which will be particularly noticeable on Econet.

Reading Text from Disc, via a Buffer: This third method is a variation on the second, which gets the data off the disc much more quickly:

> Create a temporary buffer to receive the contents of a
> file (e.g. by altering HIMEM or changing Screen Mode).
> LOAD the disc file to the buffer.
> Set a pointer to its start.
> REPEAT
> Read a string from the buffer into a string variable.
> Advance the pointer by its length, plus one.
> UNTIL the end marker is found or all string variables are filled.
> Restore HIMEM, or Screen Mode, if altered.
> Continue with the program

Example 1c: Inputting text from disc, via a buffer

With this third method, one needs to use the string indirection operator (e.g. temp\$ = \$pointer) to read strings from the buffer. This is not part of standard BASIC, but equivalents may be found in other implementations of BASIC.

By using any of these three methods, we avoid storing text in duplicate. Methods 1 and 3 involve temporary duplication, but, as long as the text is read in at the beginning of the program, the memory which is used then becomes available for other purposes. Method 2, which is slower, involves no duplication. All three can be used to fill string arrays, and they offer a substantial saving of memory, equivalent to most of the text which is read in from the disc. Other programmers may have their own favourite methods. In any BASIC program where large amounts of text cause a shortage of memory, some such solution is well worth considering.

Avoiding Wastage of Space in BASIC Strings: We come now to the way in which BASIC allots space for strings. It is well known that memory space is wasted if strings are increased in length during the course of a program. BASIC can usually cope with a limited amount of expansion (up to 8 characters, in BBC BASIC), but when a string becomes too big for the space previously allocated to it, new accommodation has to be found for it elsewhere in the memory, while the old accommodation still takes up space. This is why it is recognised as good practice to start the program by declaring strings at the maximum length which they will eventually reach. That way, new accommodation will never be needed. However, it is not always realised that, in BBC BASIC at least, this procedure itself wastes space.

A glance at Example 2 will reveal how the waste occurs. If a string of 8 or more characters is declared, such as alligator1$ in Example 2a, BBC BASIC allocates an extra 8 bytes to it, so that it can be expanded. This can be seen in Example 2b, by comparing the length of the string with the space allocated, and also in the memory dump in Example 2c. On the other hand, small strings of 1 to 7 characters are simply allocated the stated length. The result of allowing for expansion is that although we may have intended BASIC to allocate precisely 16 bytes to alligator1$, it has in fact used up 24. In order to get BASIC to use only 16 bytes, we must 'pre-shrink' the string, i.e. initially declare it at its length minus 8, as is done for alligator2$ in Example 2a.

alligator1$="like a crocodile"
alligator2$=STRING$(8,CHR$0)
alligator2$="like a crocodile"

Example 2a: BASIC program to create two strings of 16 characters

Name of string	Length	Space allocated	Overheads
alligator1$	16	24	8 PLUS 4
alligator2$	16	16	0 PLUS 4

Example 2b: The resulting use of memory

```
1A30          6C  69  6B  65  20  61  20    like a      Text of alligator1$
1A38  63  72  6F  63  6F  64  69  6C        crocodil
1A40  65  00  00  00  00  00  00  00        e.......    8 extra bytes for expansion
1A48  00  00  00

1A58          6C  69  6B  65  20  61        like a      Text of alligator2$
1A60  20  63  72  6F  63  6F  64  69          crocodi
1A68  6C  65                                le          No space for expansion
```

Example 2c: Edited dump of the strings (in hexadecimal)

Unfortunately, this represents a Pyrrhic victory for us, since it takes more than 8 bytes to make the extra declaration! For this reason, there is little that can be done as regards individual string variables, unless the program would in any case have declared them more than once. However, in the case of string arrays, particularly those with many elements, it can well be profitable to 'pre-shrink' the strings. Example 3 shows the steps which might be followed if reading text into a string array from DATA, or from disc:

> For each string in array$:
> Read a string from source into temp$.
> L = the length of temp$.
> IF L is between 9 and 15, then reset L to 8.
> If L ≥ 15, then subtract 8 from L.
> Declare array$(n) as length L.
> Re-declare array$(n) as temp$.

Example 3: 'Pre-shrinking' the strings of an array

The reason for the special treatment of lengths from 9 to 15 is that if we were simply to subtract 8, the result would be a length between 1 and 7, and BASIC would not add any bytes for expansion.

The saving that can be expected from 'pre-shrinking' the strings of an array is not as dramatic as that achieved by using disc files to create them. It can never exceed 8 bytes per string, and will be less in the case of strings of less than 16 characters. The proportionate gain is highest when many strings have a length of 16 characters or just over. Nevertheless, the device can be incorporated at little cost in any program which uses a large string array, and it can be used in conjunction with one of the disc-loading techniques to achieve a very substantial overall saving in the space needed to store text.

We stated earlier in this paper that storing text in BASIC strings is less than 50% efficient. It is possible to improve this figure greatly by using the disc drive to create the strings, by 'pre-shrinking' them, and, of course, by not leaving strings unused, such as element zero in an array. In the last case, however, only 4 bytes are wasted by leaving the string empty. The fact that every BASIC string requires at least 4 bytes of data (two for its address, one for its length and one for the space allocated), plus space for the name of the string or the array, means that however careful we are to avoid waste and duplication, storing text in BASIC strings can never be as economical as some other forms, notably what is known as pure ASCII text. Before moving on to text compression, let us look briefly at them.

3. Text Storage other than in BASIC Strings

ASCII Text: One general characteristic of what is known as ASCII text is that all the bytes represent characters (letters, spaces, punctuation marks), with the exception of line endings, which are usually marked by carriage returns (ASCII code 13 plus, in some forms, ASCII code 10). Many word-processors store text more or less in this form, but may incorporate into it their own edit commands, tab characters, etc. There are no data bytes indicating addresses and allocated space, as in BASIC strings.

When writing a CALL program, we can choose between storing text in BASIC strings, or in some form such as pure ASCII. BASIC strings, even if we use all the economising methods outlined in section 2, will always use at least three more bytes than those in pure ASCII, because the latter's single carriage return is replaced, in effect, by 4 data bytes. However, although we may save space in this way, it may take longer to find a particular line, because we have to search through the whole text instead of reading its address. In this respect, a BASIC string array provides very fast access to its elements, because their addresses are stored in a table which is stored just after the name of the array.

Pointers and Markers: Speed of access can, however, be improved if pointers are used instead or carriage returns. This means that instead of indicating the length of each string by putting a marker byte (ASCII code 13) at the end, we can precede the string by a one-byte pointer corresponding to the number of characters which it contains. Thus, instead of:

String zero[13]string one[13]string two[13]string three[13]

Example 4a: ASCII strings delimited with carriage returns

we might have:

[11]String zero[10]string one[10]string two[12]string three

Example 4b: Strings delimited by pointers indicating length

The benefit becomes apparent when we seek the start of string 3. If the ends of strings are marked by carriage returns, we might go through the following steps:

Set a pointer to the start of the text.
Set a counter to zero.

REPEAT
Read the next byte and advance the pointer
Is it a carriage return?
If so, advance the counter.
UNTIL counter = 3
Pointer now holds address of string 3

Example 4c: Searching strings with carriage returns

On the other hand, if each string is preceded by a byte indicating its length,
we might proceed as follows:

Set a pointer to the start of the text
Set a counter to zero
REPEAT
Read the number at the location indicated by pointer
Add it, plus 1, to the pointer
Advance the counter
UNTIL counter = 3
Pointer now holds address of string 3

Example 4d: Searching strings preceded by length indicators

The second procedure is not obviously quicker, but the loop is executed only three
times, whereas the loop in Example 4c is executed 34 times. The saving in access
time becomes very significant when the strings are long, and when the part of the
program which locates the string is written in machine code.

Choice of Text Storage: How, then are we to decide in what form to store text?
The choice is largely determined by the language in which the program is written.
If it is entirely in BASIC, and there are no problems of speed or of finding space to
store text, then BASIC strings and string arrays are the obvious choice. If there is
a lot of text to store, then it may be worth considering storing it in a more compact
form, and writing extra code (preferably machine code) to access it. If the language
is not BASIC, then BASIC strings are obviously out of the question.

4. Text Compression

Scope of this Survey: Text compression is such a wide subject that only the briefest
survey can be given here, and I shall limit myself to those aspects which seem relevant to language teaching on microcomputers. Many techniques have been devised,

all with the common aim of reducing the amount of space needed to store a given text. They achieve this by two principal means: utilising the computer's memory more efficiently (normal ASCII text does not use all 8 bits of every byte), and compiling dictionaries, or wordlists.

As examples of the former technique, we will outline and compare four methods which do not require much memory to implement them, and are hence suitable for small microcomputers. This means that we must ignore the complicated methods which treat memory as a 'bitstream' (a continuous line of bits which can be divided into groups of any number), and stick to those which simply subdivide the 8-bit byte into two groups of four bits, known as 'nybbles'. We will look at the amount of compression they achieve, and also at the range of ASCII codes which they offer, since the needs of modern language teaching to cope with foreign characters can add 15 or more to the character set which suffices for English. Finally, we will discuss wordlists.

Character Pairing: Character pairing (combining pairs of the 16 commonest characters into single bytes) was described by Jonathan Temple (1). This method exploits the fact that the characters which are commonest in written English (space *etaoinshrdlugcy*) often occur in pairs. Where this is the case, they are combined in a single byte in the range 64 to 255. Since this provides 192 codes (16 times 12), it means that any group of two characters, of which the first is one of the 16 commonest characters, and the second is one of the 12 commonest can be compressed into one byte. All other characters, including those common ones which cannot be paired off, are converted to values in the range 2 to 63. Since this is not enough for the normal character set, upper case letters are converted to lower case, and preceded by a flag byte with the value 1. This results in the following combinations:

NYBBLE	NYBBLE	NYBBLE	NYBBLE	
chr.	+	chr.		(*etaoinshrdlugcy* + *etaoinshrdlugcy*)
	chr.			(other lower case chrs.)
	flag	chr.	+	chr.	(*ETAOINSHRDLUGCY* + *etaoinshrdlugcy*)
	flag	chr.		(other upper case chrs.)

Example 5a: Character pairing (character patterns)

The process of compressing the text can be summarised as follows:

---

(1) *The Micro User*, October 1986.

REPEAT FOR EACH CHARACTER:
If upper case, convert to lower case; output a flag byte
If chr. is (now) one of 16 common chrs...
    And if next chr. is one of 12 common chrs...
    Then combine them in a byte in range 64 - 255 and output the byte
    Else convert to range 2 to 63; output the byte
UNTIL ALL THE TEXT IS PROCESSED

Example 5b: Character pairing (compression method)

Thus, when the text is later unpacked, numbers in the range 64 to 255 are expanded into two characters, and characters preceded by a flag byte are converted to upper case. The use of this flag byte represents a gamble, since it causes one letter to be represented by two bytes. They are (usually) relatively rare, however, and the loss will be compensated by the compression achieved by pairing, and the fact that ETAOINSHRDLUGCY, once converted to lower case, become eligible for pairing. Nevertheless, a large number of capitals in a text causes a marked reduction in compression, and could in exceptional cases lead to the 'compressed' text being much longer than the original. Only 88 characters are provided (not enough for languages such as French), but the flag byte could be further exploited to modify other characters, so that the total set could be increased to 124 (62 'plain', and 62 preceded by a flag). Nonetheless, care should be taken to ensure that only the rarer characters need a flag byte.

Dealing with Combinations of 4 and 8 Bits: Since the remaining three methods involve using mixtures of 4 and 8 bits, with the result that a 'letter' can straddle the gap between 2 bytes, it may be helpful here to outline a simple algorithm for adding characters to the text already compressed. We will assume that the result is sent out to a disc file, byte by byte. We will use one byte (W) as a 'waiting-room' to store a single nybble until the rest of the byte can be filled; and one flag (Wflag) to signify that the 'waiting-room' is occupied.

To add a character of 4 bits, or 1 nybble (N):

    If Wflag is CLEAR, store N* 16 in W; set Wflag
    If SET, add N to W and output W; clear Wflag

To add a character of 8 bits, or 1 byte (B):

If Wflag is CLEAR, output B

If SET, (a) add upper nybble of B (B DIV 16) to W; output W

(b) store lower nybble of B (B* 16 AND 240) in W

Example 6: Adding 4-bit and 8-bit units to a compressed text

Any mention which we may make in the next three sections of outputting 4- and 8-bit characters should be taken as reference to this.

4:8 Bit Compression: This method was described by Peter Finch (2), following an article in the *Journal of the British Computing Society*. It subdivides all bytes into 4-bit nybbles, each capable of signifying a number in the range 0 to 15. Value 0 indicates a space; values 1 to 9 indicate the common characters *aeiorstln* respectively; values 10 to 15 indicate that the next 4 bits must also be read, and that their value (in the range 0 to 15) must be added, respectively, to 32, 48, 64, 80, 96 or 112. Thus, characters are represented by 4 or 8 bits (i.e. 1 or 2 nybbles):

NYBBLE	NYBBLE	
chr.		(space, *aeiorstln*)
flag	chr.	(all other chrs.)

Example 7a: 4:8 bit compression (character patterns)

The process of compression can be summarised as follows:

REPEAT FOR EACH CHARACTER:

If it is one of the 10 common chrs,

then output a 4-bit number (0 to 9)

Else make sure ASCII code is in range 32 to 127;

divide ASCII code by 16;

output quotient PLUS 8 (10 to 15 as a 4-bit flag)

output the remainder as a 4-bit number

UNTIL ALL THE TEXT IS PROCESSED

Example 7b: 4:8 bit compression (method)

As a result of this method, the characters which occur most commonly only occupy half a byte. The range of characters is quite good: the 'normal' set of 96 is increased, since the ten common characters are represented outside the normal system. This

---

(2) *Personal Computer World*, May, 1985.

means that their usual ASCII codes can be utilised for other purposes. Two are in fact used as carriage return and end-of-text marker, but the overall total of 104 leaves enough room to create at least 15 foreign characters, if redundant symbols such as # <>, etc., are also utilised.

4:8:12:16 Bit Compression: This method, which is intended for use in adventure games, is described by Peter Gerrard (3). As the author does not give it a name, we will refer to it as 4:8:12:16 bit compression. It is essentially an extension of simple 4:8 bit compression: the 14 commonest characters (space, *etonairshldcu*) are represented by a 4-bit number (0 to 13), and 29 others (*pwmgyfbvkzzjq'* in one group, *0123456789!?;.,* in a second group) by 4-bit numbers (0 to 14) preceded by 4-bit flags (14 or 15, according to the group). This allows a total of only 43 characters (26 lower case letters, numerals and common punctuation signs). In addition, upper case letters can be represented (as in the case of character pairing) by preceding the lower case code (which could be 4 or 8 bits) with an 8-bit flag. This gives a very restricted total character set of 69, leaving no room for such things as quotation marks and per cent symbols, let alone foreign characters. However, the system could be modified (in the same way as character pairing) to bring the total up to 88 — still not enough for many foreign languages. The possible ways of representing characters are as follows:

NYBBLE	NYBBLE	NYBBLE	NYBBLE
chr.			
flag +	chr.		
flag	+	chr.	
flag	+	flag +	chr.

(space, *etonairshldcu*)
(*pwmgyfbvkzzjq'*) *0123456789!?;.,*)
(*ETONAIRSHLDCU*)
(*PWMGYFBVKXZJQ*)

Example 8: 4:8:12:16 bit compression (character patterns)

Although a compression rate of around 58% is claimed by its author, this ignores carriage returns, and the many characters which have to be omitted because they are not within the acceptable range. As in the case of character pairing, the efficiency declines markedly when the text contains many upper case letters. The overall performance is thus broadly similar to that of character pairing, but the character set is much smaller.

4:8:12 Bit Compression: In order to meet the requirements of CALL programmes with foreign characters, we suggest here a fourth method, which combines some of the virtues of the above three with the ability to accept a large character set (256 with a possible extension to 286). Compression is achieved in two stages:

---

(3) *The Micro User*, (1987), September, pp.102 - 105.

(1) The text is checked to discover the 30 commonest characters
(2) The compression process itself

The first stage is not essential, but can improve efficiency. It also costs virtually nothing in terms of memory, because the work is done prior to the actual compression. It is advisable because the frequency of characters varies not only from one language to another, but from one text to another: a frequency check on a list of dictionary headwords will produce a different result from one on a colloquial passage from a novel, or a technical passage with statistics. The check can be done as follows:

> Initialise 256 counters
> Go through text, counting each ASCII code
> Sort the counters into order of frequency

Now for the second stage. The aim is to represent the 14 commonest characters (as indicated by the list which was established in Stage 1) by 4-bit numbers (0 to 13). The next 16 commonest characters are represented by 4-bit numbers (0 to 15) preceded by a 4-bit flag (value: 14). All other characters remain as normal 8-bit ASCII codes, preceded by 4-bit flags (value: 15). The possible combinations are:

NYBBLE	NYBBLE	NYBBLE
chr.			(14 commonest chrs.)
flag	chr.		(next 16 commonest)
flag	+	chr.	(all other chrs.)

Example 9a 4:8:12 bit compression (character patterns)

The process of compression is as follows:

(1) Output the list of the 30 commonest characters to the disc file.
(2) REPEAT FOR EACH CHARACTER:

> If one of the 14 commonest, output a 4-bit number (0 to 13)
> If among the 16 next commonest, (a) output a 4-bit flag (14)
>   (b) output a 4-bit number (0 to 15)
> Otherwise, (a) output a 4-bit flag (15)
>   (b) output the 8-bit ASCII code of the chr.

UNTIL ALL THE TEXT IS PROCESSED

(*Example 9a*: 4:8:12 bit compression (method))

The character set of 256 can be extended, if desired, because the normal ASCII codes of the 30 commonest characters are no longer used. Apart from the range of characters, another virtue of this method, compared with character pairing and 4:8:12:16 bit compression, is that the presence of rarer letters (e.g. upper case or foreign) does less harm to the rate of compression because they never occupy more than 12 bits, whereas the latter two methods use 16 bits.

The Four Methods Compared: All save space by representing the commonest characters by only 4 bits. All are capable (given a suitable text) of achieving a compression of just under two-thirds (i.e. the original text is reduced to two-thirds of its length): around 62-63% is claimed for character pairing, and 65 - 66% for 4:8 bit compression. Around 58% is claimed for 4:8:12:16 bit compression, but when carriage returns are counted in (as in the other methods), this reduces to 61 - 62%, and would reach at least 66% if the character set were extended to a range comparable to that of the others.

The yield can vary according to the text, particularly in the case of character pairing and 4:8:12:16 bit compression. A sample text (the first part of this paper) was compressed by each method, then several sentences were put into upper case, and the test was repeated. The results are:

Character pairing	64.7%
4:8 bit	65.7%
4:8:12:16 bit	61.9%*
4:8:12 bit	63.6%

Example 10a: Comparison of compression ratios

*This figure ignores the characters (129 bytes) which were omitted because they were outside the acceptable range. If the system were modified to include each in the same way as upper case letters, the compression rate would be 71.4%.

However, when the same text, with several sentences put into upper case, is compressed in the same way, the results are:

Character pairing	90.4%
4:8 bit	72.5%
4:8:12:16 bit	82%*
4:8:12 bit	75.2%

*If the character is extended, this becomes 91.5%.

Example 10b: Another comparison of compression ratios

In the case of 'normal' text the compression ratios achieved by each method were roughly in line with the claims of their authors. When the text contained more upper case letters, the yield dropped slightly in the second and fourth methods, and sharply in the case of first and third. It can thus be seen that all lose efficiency when there are fewer 'compressible' characters, and that methods which use two bytes to represent some letters suffer more than others. As to the question of which is the most satisfactory, it all depends on the nature of the text, and the range of characters required. The answer will only be found by careful study of the text, or by experiment.

Wordlists: Long texts can be compressed by compiling a wordlist (sometimes also called a dictionary) and recording the text itself as a series of numbers which refer to the words in the list. Given an average word length of about 5.9 characters, and assuming that we use 2 bytes to replace each word, this gives a compression to 33% of the original — *if* we disregard the space taken by the wordlist itself. However, when the latter is taken into consideration, it becomes clear that wordlists only become an economical proposition if the text is very long, or contains many repetitions. On the other hand, they offer the advantage of greater speed in handling text, as was pointed out by Brian Farrington at the 1985 Exeter Conference (4).

We will briefly describe the results of using wordlists in a language teaching program which is currently being developed at Bangor, called *Apicale*. By writing the program itself in machine code, it was possible to reserve just over 10K of the available 16K of memory for the text of the exercises. This proved adequate in most cases, so the first two versions stored text on the basis of 1 byte per character. However, although the program itself could cope with up to 256 possible answers to each question, each of up to 200 characters, it is obvious that memory shortage would occur if many questions had many possible long answers. Fortunately, this rarely occurs, but it would nonetheless be useful to have the capacity to cope with

---

(4) cf. Brian Farrington, "A Micro-computer program for checking translation at sentence level", Language Laboratory, University of Aberdeen.

such an eventuality.

The problem is caused by what can be called 'branching'. At several points in the sentence, two or more possibilities present themselves. Each time, the total number of possible sentences is multiplied by 2 or more. Hence, one passes very rapidly from 8 to 16, 32, 64, and so on. One solution which was investigated was to record the actual branching of the sentence, as in the following translation(s) of the English sentence, 'As he ran down the road, the boy thought he heard his grandmother telling his sister to fetch him before it got dark':

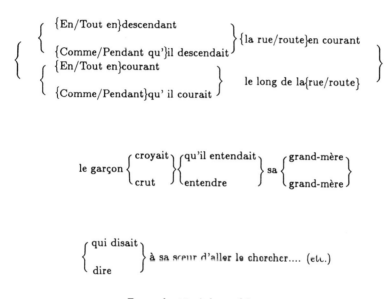

Example 11: A branching sentence

This approach, which can be compared with that adopted in Brian Farrington's excellent program *Littré*, was abandoned for two reasons: (1) it made both programming and writing the exercises complicated; (2) it seemed desirable to let the teacher review each possible sentence as a whole, and eliminate certain combinations which appeared unlikely. For instance, in the above example, the formal-sounding *crut entendre* might have stylistic implications which affect choices elsewhere in the sentence. Hence it was decided to write the text on a word-processor, and store it more or less in that form in versions 1 and 2 of the program, but to use wordlists in version 3. Despite the relative shortness of the texts, wordlists are feasible because sentences with many variations inevitably contain many repetitions.

This version is presently in the testing stage, but it is already apparent that the text compression which is achieved varies greatly, according to the nature of the text, as can be seen in Example 9. For the sake of comparison, we also give the compression achieved by using 4:8:12 bit compression (the only method available which copes with the wide character range).

TEXT OF EXERCISE	ORIGINAL LENGTH	COMPRESSION (a) wordlists	USING (b) 4:8:12 bit
Brief introduction, then sentences	10063	59%	60.8%
Brief introduction, then sentences	10355	67%	62.2%
Text and comprehension questions (answers in French)	9702	86%	62.7%
Literary passage and phonetic transcription	5897	87%	71.7%
Grammatical explanation (agreement of the past participle), then sentences	7156	88%	66.1%

Example 12: Results of compressing some *Apicale* exercises

Although the ratios for wordlist compression do not match what can be achieved by techniques such as the 4:8:12 bit method, its use proves profitable because it brings relief where relief is most needed, namely in those exercises where multiple branching greatly increases the number of possible answers. Putting it another way, the longer the text, the greater the usefulness of wordlists.

A major advantage of wordlists over other compression techniques is the accessibility of individual elements within the text as a whole. When characters are represented by groups of 4 and 8 bits, the end of a letter (and sometimes of a word) does not always coincide with the end of a byte. This causes no problem when the text merely needs to be displayed, from start to finish, on the screen, as in the case of the directions in an adventure game; but it makes the task of matching a given student's answer with the possible models extremely slow and difficult. Wordlists, on the other hand, make this task extremely fast, because all words can be accessed separately, and the compressed text consists of a regular succession of 2-byte addresses.

The efficiency of wordlists can be enhanced by various additional compression techniques. It is common practice to omit the first letter of each word in the list, and, instead, mark the start of groups which begin with initial A,B,C,a,b,c, etc. Other ways of compressing wordlists are described in the Appendix to this paper: they are mostly unsuitable to short wordlists, and restrict the character set to a degree which would be unacceptable in modern language teaching.

5. *Conclusions*

To sum up: there is considerable scope for more economical text storage in CALL. If the more ambitious programs run out of memory, the solution need not necessarily be in buying a second processor or a bigger computer. Careful use of BASIC strings can halve the text storage requirements. Text compression techniques can be applied to programs in both BASIC and in machine code, and may bring other advantages such as greater speed.

Comparing wordlists, as a compression technique, with other techniques, one can see clear attractions as regards CALL. One is that this method does not restrict the number of ASCII codes which can be used. This means that other alphabets, such as Cyrillic or phonetic symbols, can be present in the same compressed text as the conventional Latin alphabet. On the other hand, certain other methods, such as 4:8:12 bit compression, can cope with the same range of characters. The main advantage of wordlists is that text handling is speeded up, because all words are uniformly reduced to two bytes. This is particularly valuable when comparing student answers against large numbers of possible models. On the other hand, wordlists require a considerable initial outlay, in terms of memory, and are not really economical for shorter texts.

The usefulness of any method of text compression in CALL programs can only be assessed in the light of the nature of the text and the requirements of the character set.

Appendix

Wordlist compression techniques in spelling checkers

(a) Compressed wordlists in *Spellmaster*: The first letter is indicated by group header (&81 = end of A and start of initial letter B); the second letter has bits 6 and 7 set, to mark the start of a new word (or the end of previous one). SAVING: 2 bytes per word.

50	45	43	54	53	D4	D6	41	PECTS..A	[as]pects
49	4C	41	42	4C	45	D6	4F	ILABLE.O	[av]ailable [av]oid
49	44	81	C1	53	45	44	C1	ID..SED.B.	[ba]sed
53	49	43	C2	43	C5	C5	43	SIC.C..C	[ba]sic [BB]C
41	55	53	45	C5	43	4F	4D	AUSE.COM	[be]cause [be]comes

The character set is restricted to upper case letters.

(b) Compressed wordlists in *Viewspell*: Three compression techniques are employed. Initial letters are omitted. About 160 common suffixes are denoted by single bytes in the range 91 - 255. In this way, for example, fifteen words beginning [b]as- could be stored in 17 bytes:

     [b]as/e/es/ed/er/est/al/s/ing/ic/ics/ely/eness/eless /ement/ically

Finally, where a word begins with the same series of letters as the previous word in the list, ASCII codes 1 - 31 indicate how many letters are in common, e.g.:

     [s]upper
     [s][upp]lant
     [s][uppl]e
     [s][uppl]y
     [s][upp]ort
     [s][uppo]se (5)

---

(5) See: Rob Macmillan, (1986),"Spell it out", in *Acorn User*, October.

VI

AI: 'GRANDEUR' OR 'SERVITUDE'?

Brian Farrington

University of Aberdeen

1. The End of a Phase for CALL

The development of Computer Assisted Language Learning is at the moment coming to the end of one chapter, and the start of another. Three features of this transitional phase can be distinguished:

Firstly, regrettable or no, there can be no denying that the novelty which was a principal motivator both of teacher and learner can no longer be counted on. The market for computer games, like that for small home computers, has shrunk, maybe because of the greater status of the more powerful PC clones now appearing in high street shops, but maybe also for the simpler reason that nothing can remain new for long, and the limited resources of the home computer and the *Space Invader* had been exhausted. Whatever the reason, it is likely that the argument for CALL that was based on its motivating power ("They are enjoying themselves", a teacher once said to me, of his class, happily zapping irregular verbs, "and what they are doing is French") is now wearing thin. CALL programs will soon, if this is not already true, only motivate if they are challenging, perplexing, and interesting in themselves, like any other language learning activity.

Secondly, the wave of innovation which marked the decade of DIY CALL seems to have passed. Several years have gone by without the appearance of a second *Storyboard* (1) or *Jumbler* (2). Ideas for new types of CALL materials have been thin on the ground for some time. Where interesting innovations are being made it is in the field rather of methodology and of application, such as with *Micro-Concord*, (3) where the computer plays an essential, liberating and enabling role, but as an

---

(1) Higgins, J., (1982), *Storyboard*, Wida Software.
(2) Johns, T., (1981), "The uses of an analytic generator: the computer as teacher of English for specific purposes", *ELT Documents 112*. The British Council.
(3) Johns, T., (1986), "Micro-Concord: a Language Learners' Research Tool", *System*. **14,2.**

instrument, an accessory to the business of learning. (When used in this way the computer is, precisely, assisting learning. It is a point worth bearing in mind.)

There is also some evidence of a general disenchantment with CALL on the part of teachers. Jenny Thomas refers to this, (4) saying that "Classroom language teachers and applied linguists alike are expressing serious doubts about the pedagogical value of CALL programs". Though Ms Thomas gives no references to justify her remarks about "the main thrust of teachers' criticisms", it is true that evidence of a negative kind is not hard to discover. CALL has not taken off, few publishers include more than a few CALL packages in their lists, and sales of these are slow. After 10 years of development it is still the affair of a relatively tiny minority of enthusiasts only.

Thirdly, and most obviously, the nature of the currently available hardware is already undergoing a change. At the close of the 1970s a wide variety of roughly comparable microcomputers were to be found in educational institutions: Spectrums, Apples, Commodore PETs, NewBrains and RM380Z, almost all of them to be replaced in the 1980s by the ubiquitous BBC Micro. During that period the major problem faced by anyone developing CALL materials was that of compatibility. In the last few years, as Acorn came to dominate the educational field, the problem grew less and less important. It has now given way to a new *angoisse*, as the 8-bit micro becomes a piece of yesterday's technology: by what new, more powerful, and above all more expensive, 16-bit machine is it to be replaced?

The challenge of the 16-bit machine is more than a simple economic problem, however, and the possibilities it opens up are qualitatively different from those offered by the simpler equipment. It is not just a matter of having more memory to play round with: the more sophisticated machine calls for more sophisticated programming. The day of DIY CALL, of the hobbyist programmer, the teacher-enthusiast presenting his class on Monday morning with the exercise he has spent the weekend programming, may be over. We are moving into an entirely new phase, the most distinctive feature of which is sure to be the appearance on the scene of Intelligent Tutoring Systems or ITS for language learning, Intelligent CALL.

2. Intelligent CALL

What does this term 'Intelligent CALL' mean? One is tempted to reply simply that it just stands for CALL materials written by computer scientists instead of being

---

(4) Thomas, J., (1986), "Adapting dBase II: The use of Database Management Systems in English Language Teaching and Research", in Leech, G. and Candlin, C. (Eds), (1986), *Computers in English Language Teaching and Research*, Longman.

written by language teachers or linguists, or that it just means CALL materials with programs in PROLOG or LISP instead of BASIC. For the purposes of this paper I will assume that the label 'intelligent CALL' can be fairly applied to any exercise in which an attempt is made to get the system to process language in a way that approximates, *or appears to approximate*, to that used by human beings. I say "attempt is being made" because the whole thing is still very tentative. Although descriptions of several ITSs for language learning are to be found in the literature, (5) these are still at the experimental stage. As yet I know of no intelligent language teaching system in regular everyday use by students, by which I mean in the course of their normal activity, and without a researcher breathing down their necks and looking over their shoulders.

However, great things are promised of this new phase: Yazdani in a recent conference paper has spoken of "powerful teaching systems aiming to be as competent as a good human teacher". It is the aim of this paper to suggest some of the points that will have to be borne in mind when these powerful teaching systems come to deal seriously with that most intractable, and as yet only partly understood, phenomenon, that is natural language.

Before continuing, though, I think a word should be said in defence, and in praise, of the DIY teacher-programmer, whom, I suspect it will soon be fashionable to look down on. It is easy for pundits to sneer: the term 'hobbyist', used by Thomas, strikes me as offensively pejorative. John Self has written a stinging criticism (6) (cf. for example, Chapter 19 The Institutionalisation of Mediocrity) of current educational software, for the most part produced by suchlike 'hobbyists', or 'tcp's, (teacher-cum-programmer). Now, it is certainly true that there is plenty of

---

(5) See:Cerri, S. and Breuker, J., (1981), "A rather intelligent language teacher", *Studies in Language Learning*, 3, 182-192; Emirkanian, L. and Bouchard, L., (1987), "Exploitation des Connaissances de la Langue dans la Création d'un Didacticiel", Mimeo, Paper presented at EAO87 Conference, France, 1987; Last, R.W., (1986) "Potential of Artificial Intelligence-Related CALL at the Sentence Level", *Journal of the Association for Literary and Linguistic Computing*; Markosian, L.Z. and Ager, T.A., (1983), "Applications of parsing theory to computer-assisted language instruction", *System*. 11, 1, 65-77; Sampson, G., (1986) "Transition Networks for Computer-Assisted Language Learning", in Leech and Candlin (1986); Schwind, C., (1987), "Un Système Expert pour l'Enseignement Assisté par Ordinateur des Langues Etrangères", Mimeo, Paper presented at EAO87 Conference, France; Ward, R.D., (1986), "Natural language processing and the language impaired", *Programmed Learning and Educational Technology*, 23, 2, pp.144-149; Weischedel, R.M., Voge, W. M., and James, M., (1978), "An Artificial Intelligence Approach to Language Instruction", *Artificial Intelligence*, 10, 225-240.

(6) Self, J., (1985), *Microcomputers in Education*, Harvester Press.

poor quality CALL material about, though it is interesting to note that none of Self's examples are taken from the field of foreign language learning. It is, nevertheless, also true that much of the software produced in this country for language learning, and by 'tcp's, outshines in innovative ingenuity and linguistic insight most of the work done abroad, and is cited for these qualities by foreign experts (7). Also, if the next generation of CALL materials does take off, it will depend upon the existence of a body of computerate language teachers. That such a thing should exist is largely because of the DIY phase of CALL development. What is more, materials produced by teachers for Spectrum or BBC micro (8) have the virtue of being conceived at the 'chalk face'. It is a virtue that should not be too sweepingly dismissed, as we move into the rarefied atmosphere of AI.

What are the principal aims of an intelligent tutoring system for language learning? For Yazdani (9) such a system should know the subject it is proposing to teach, in this case the grammar of the language taught. It should be capable of user-modelling and therefore offer truly individualised instruction. The learner, in fact, should not be obliged to follow any pre-ordained pattern of instruction. And the system should be able to learn from the learner, both about the subject and about the problems of learning it. In place of the dumb procrustean framework of the conventional CALL exercise, an intelligent system would create a "reactive learning environment" (10) in which the learner would be able to carry on a free natural dialogue *in* the language, as well as *about* the language that she was learning.

It is difficult to test such claims, since there are as yet no intelligent language teaching programs in regular use anywhere. There are, however, several already in existence and running, though still only experimentally. In an earlier paper, (11) I examined two such systems in detail, one (12) dating from 10 years ago and one (13) very recent. Both are designed to teach German to near beginners. In the first the system presents a short text and then questions the learner about its content,

(7) Demaizière, F., (1986), *Enseignement Assisté par Ordinateur*, Editions Ophrys, Paris.

(8) Adams, J. and Adams, P., (1984), "Computers and French", *Modern Languages in Scotland*, SCDS, Edinburgh.

(9) See *infra*, Chapter VIII.

(10) Brown, J.S., Burton, R.R., Bell, A.G., (1975), "SOPHIE: A Step Toward Creating a Reactive Learning Environment", *Int Journal of Man-Machine Studies*, 7.

(11) Farrington, B., (1987), "Is the intelligent artefact a rotten teacher?", in Ager, D., (ED) (1987), *Written Skills in the Undergraduate Curriculum*, CILT.

(12) Weischedel, R.M., Voge, W.M., and James, M., (1978), "An Artificial Intelligence Approach to Language Instruction", *Artificial Intelligence*, 10, 225-240.

(13) Schwind, C., (1987), "Un Système Expert pour l'Enseignement Assisté par Ordinateur des Langues Etrangères", Mimeo, Paper presented at EAO87 Conference, France.

analysing the answers and commenting on mistakes made. The second puts a list of words on the screen and invites the learner to compose a sentence using a selection of them. The aim of both systems is similar: it is to monitor the production of sentences in 'correct' German, that is to say sentences without formal grammar or syntactic mistakes. In both these systems we can see many of the advantages of the more sophisticated approach actually working. The learner is free to use language naturally, s/he is in no way locked into a preordained sequence of operations, filling in slots or having his/her responses matched to a finite set of right or wrong answers. With Dr Schwind's program the learner is free to interrogate the system, asking for explanations or exercises, or proposing sentences which the system then analyses and criticises. It follows that no two sessions with the system need be the same.

3. Inadequacies of Present Intelligent Systems

Though the perspectives opened up by the mere existence of such systems seem impressive, their limitations are considerable, but the shortcomings are not a matter of mere physical resources. If it were so then we could be confident that in a few years' time the technology will have presented us with equipment that will leave these precursors far behind. Rather, what these powerful new tutoring systems do is to highlight by their very efficiency the inadequacies of the model of language-learning that lies, not only behind their sophisticated programming, but also behind a considerable amount of conventional current CALL materials. As has been pointed out (14) CALL "is a medium that reveals the methodological assumptions of its authors with unusual clarity". If this is true of steam-driven 'dumb' CALL how much more true it must be of an intelligent system? Maybe this will turn out to be the most valuable contribution that AI has made so far.

To start off, we will deal with what may seem to some to be a trivial point: the importance attached to mistakes and correctness. The so-called grammar-translation method was a methodology of error-correction. The basic assumption was of a finite body of knowledge — the language — existing somewhere outside the teaching/learning situation, and imperfectly possessed by the learner. Instruction, when it took place, was based on the mistakes a learner was liable to make negotiating the various 'difficulties' anticipated by the teacher. The learner was then invited to perform in the language, to see how many holes s/he would fall into in doing so. The more of these holes the learner fell into, the more mistakes s/he made, the more the method seemed justified. The main teaching activity then consisted of correcting the mistakes made. The whole approach was essentially neg-ative, and it was impossible to grade the errors in order of gravity or importance, except subjectively, by the teacher.

(14) Wyatt, D., (1984), *Computers and ESL*, Harcourt Brace and Jovanovich.

It will be objected, and rightly, that I am here misrepresenting the grammar-translation method. Of course no human teacher would ever have proceeded exactly in this way. But what I have in fact just described is the procedure adopted by numerous drill and practice CALL exercises, including most of the would-be intelligent tutoring systems cited, several of which are, essentially, mere error-checkers. It is an approach that might well be successful for teaching someone to write a dead language, or a computer programming language. It hardly can be said to fit any intuitions about the manner in which natural language is acquired.

I remarked above on the manner in which a more powerful system highlights more clearly the inadequacy of the model of language-learning adopted. There is a clear example of this in the matter of formal grammatical accuracy. The polarisation of accuracy and fluency, underlined by Brumfit, (15) means that the teacher must select activities in such a way as to favour neither aspect overmuch, for fear of neglecting the other. The two are not equal, as far as the ultimate aim of the learning is concerned. Brumfit points out (16):

> Language display for evaluation tended to lead to a concern for accuracy, monitoring, reference rules, possibly explicit knowledge, problem solving and evidence of skill-getting. In contrast, language use requires fluency, expression rules, a reliance on implicit knowledge and automatic performance.

In other words, accuracy is important in examinations, but "in the kind of natural circumstances for which teaching (is) presumably a preparation" it is fluency that is required. Good teaching will of course lay emphasis on both, but in the end the one that matters most is fluency. In these circumstances the appearance on the scene of a high-powered, artificially intelligent accuracy promoter can only underline the shortcomings of an approach to language learning that accords to the achievement of correctness a priority over fluency in language use.

The question may seem to be one of only secondary significance. It is, however, a surface symptom of an underlying inadequacy of much greater importance, namely the way in which the system deals, or fails to deal, with meaning. Only one of the intelligent systems listed above, and very few pre-intelligent systems, is capable of handling meaning in anything but the crudest possible of ways, i.e. by simple translation equivalence.

---

(15) Brumfit, C., (1984), *Communicative Methodology in Language Teaching*, CUP.
(16) *Ibidem*, p.51.

There are some people, of course, who will maintain that further progress in the direction of semantic complexity is impossible, that the term Artificial Intelligence is self-contradictory, that human language cannot be processed by machines in any but the most trivial and superficial of ways. For such people the only direction in which CALL, intelligent or stupid, can advance is towards ever more efficient training in the manipulation of the surface features of language. If this were true it would, in the opinion of many applied linguists, mean relegating CALL to the status of a marginal and largely futile activity. I do not share this view: I do not believe that language is infinitely, mysteriously, complex and inscrutable, and that it cannot, in theory at any rate, be understood by a machine. On the other hand I am convinced that, before any significant progress can be made, it is essential that we come to terms with what language is and what it is not.

Three-quarters of a century of linguistic science have all the same given us considerable insight into the phenomenon. Looking at some CALL materials, both intelligent and unintelligent, with their horse-drawn semantics, their concentration on morphological or syntactic rectitude, reminiscent of the old days of grammar-translation, one sees little evidence that those 75 years ever happened.

It is certainly not impossible, in the present state of the technology, to go some way towards the processing of meaningful language (17). What is worrying about the few tentative examples of Intelligent Language Tutoring systems that exist so far, as indeed about plenty of conventional materials, is, firstly, that they make little attempt in this direction, and, secondly and more seriously, that they do not seem to consider this important. One has only to look at some of the sentences generated by certain of the experimental intelligent systems mentioned, or selected by their authors for processing, to find forceful illustration of these points:

Der Schüler antwortet dem Lehrer (18)
Les voisins bavards donnent les bonbons aux petits enfants (19)
Le bateau est sorti par mon frère qui portera le pain pour le manger (20)
Der Vater des jungen Schülers überreicht ihm viele Geschenke (21)

---

(17) Sparck Jones, K., (1987), "Natural Language Processing", in O'Shea, T., Self, J., & Thomas, G., *Intelligent Knowledge-Based Systems*, Harper & Row.
(18) Schwind (1987).
(19) Emirkanian & Bouchard (1987).
(20) Imlah, W.G. and du Boulay, J.B.H., (1985), "Robust natural language parsing in computer-assisted language instruction", *System* 13, 2, 137-149.
(21) Last (1986).

Thirty years ago J.R. Firth (22) insisted on the importance of what he called the "implication of utterance". A piece of language that lacked the implication of utterance, for which there was no context, real or readily imaginable, (Edward Sapir's phrase "the farmer kills the duckling" was cited by Firth as an example) has, quite literally, no meaning. The same could be said of the sentences above. Incidentally, quite apart from the semantic oddity of these concoctions, one might add that they are all straight declarative sentences. Normal language in action consists of varied sentence types with frequent minor sentences. It is enough to compare these uncontextualisable phrases with those occurring in any standard language course for beginners (Digame, A Vous La France, Fast Forward), or indeed in any recorded conversation, to see how abnormal they are.

Manipulation of a series of meaningless sentences, as we all learnt in the language laboratories of 30 years ago, is a sterile and largely unprofitable activity. The idea of contextualisation, slogan of the last innovators of the language lab era, has, however lost none of its relevance. Why should the introduction of information technology mean that we forget the essential fact that, to quote Lyons (1981) "Meaningfulness is essential to languages as we know them; and it is arguable that the very notion of a language without meaning is logically incoherent" (23).

Almost all of the ITSs referred to, in common with many conventional systems, betray a naïve attitude towards meaning, seeing it as a feature of language that can largely be ignored, since it is something that exists beside, or outside, language. It needs to be underlined that meaning is *not* an appendage to language, existing independently of it. Rather, language *is* meaning; learning a language is, in Halliday's phrase, learning how to mean, and to learn a foreign language is to learn how to mean in a new way. The essential principle underlying most modern approaches to language learning, and uniting such disparate phenomena as the notional/functional school (24) and humanistic methods such as the *Silent Way*, indeed the whole movement behind communicative methodology, is a restatement of the importance of meaningfulness in language learning.

Such a principle is not incompatible with CALL. As an example one has only to point to the work of the ORDI team at the University of Paris VII, who have produced an impressive volume of CALL materials based on the theory of 'opérations énonciatives' of A. Culioli. The theory, (25) which is widely influential in French linguistics, expresses a view of language as 'a communicable form of thought', and

(22) Firth, J.R., (1957), *Papers in Linguistics 1934 — 1951*, OUP.
(23) Lyons, J., (1981), *Language, Meaning & Context*, Fontana.
(24) Wilkins, D., (1976), *Notional Syllabuses*, OUP.
(25) Bronckart, J.-P., (1977), *Théories du Langage, Une Introduction Critique*, Brussels.

can be placed somewhere between the Chomskian view of language as transparent, and that of J R Searle: words, linguistic forms and patterns, according to Culioli, do not *have* meanings, rather, utterances take on meaning to the extent that the operations that they effect are differentiated, and the meanings which can be associated with words are derived from the situational function of these operations. The ORDI materials (26) are exclusively tutorial, didactic, to use their own word, and might seem excessively so in British eyes. They contain a great deal of explanatory text, and they are all constructed using one, albeit powerful, authoring system. Yet neither examples nor explanations ever lose sight of the principle that language is essentially meaningful.

It can obviously be objected that drill and practice will always have some place in language learning, that contextualisation is unnecessary when it is a question simply of the mechanical practising of conditioned syntactic patterns, in short that not all language practice *has* to be meaningful. This may be true. However, there would be little point in trying to develop ambitious intelligent systems if they were only good to be used as automatic grammar grinders, a very minor sideshow to the main business of learning a language. The argument is, therefore, an irrelevancy.

On the other hand it could be said that the fault of the systems criticised is not so much that they deal in meaningless language as that they deal with levels and functions of language where meaning is important, but ignore it. It is true that there are areas of linguistic patterning where meaning is not a relevant factor at all; an example is noun gender in French. In an earlier paper, (27) After describing the disastrously counter-productive effect of a conventional CALL exercise designed to teach this explicitly, I outlined a way in which the native speaker's skill with noun gender might be modelled. Derrick Ferney in this volume (28) describes just such a program. There are certainly other areas of language where the power of the computer to process large volumes of data can reveal similar patterns and regularities which are no less powerful for being only dimly apprehended by the conscious mind. The existence of such phenomena in no way diminishes the importance of meaningfulness in language learning.

4. Possible Ways Forward

It is actually because of the importance of meaning in language learning that we need

(26) Demaizière (1986).
(27) Farrington, B., (1986), "Computer Assisted Learning or Computer Inhibited Acquisition?", in Cameron, K, Dodd, W S, and Rahtz, S P Q, (Eds), (1986), *Computers and Modern Language Studies*, Ellis Horwood.
(28) See *supra*, Chapter II.

more powerful computers, more sophisticated programming techniques, in short, intelligent systems. This is doubly true if any progress is to be made in systems for advanced learners, and I am convinced that this is where progress is both most worthwhile and most urgently needed. From the start, the natural tendency has, of course, been to concentrate on producing materials for learners at the earliest stages, and the pioneering constructors of intelligent systems mentioned above are no exception. Almost every one of the examples of experimental ITSs listed above are designed with beginners in mind. It is easy to see why: there is the idea that the language used by learners in the early stages is semantically simpler, and the implicit view that, at this stage in the learning process, meaning can be ignored, as described above. This is certainly not so, even for beginners, and, since the problem of processing meaningful language is not one that will conveniently solve itself with time, there is no point in ignoring it: the challenge must be met.

In any case there are several well-rehearsed reasons why beginners are the learners least suited to CALL work, and least likely to profit by it. The most obvious reason is of course the emphasis that must be laid on fluency in speech with learners at the early stages of learning a foreign language, while CALL is above all relevant to learning the written code. Also, the teachers of beginners are the ones least in need of computer assistance, precisely because of the importance of oral rather than written practice at this stage. The teacher of intermediate and advanced students, on the other hand, can only give her/his learners adequate practice by setting large quantities of written work and correcting it afterwards, in a sequence of operations, which, for all it is time-honoured, has little to commend it, being tedious for the teacher and unprofitable for the student. Computer exercises that would ease this effort on both sides, and increase its efficiency, would therefore answer a real need.

The problem of processing meaningful language for advanced learners remains, however, and the situation is unlikely to change. In what direction, therefore, is progress most likely to be possible? Since there is no prospect of achieving the full mimicry or modelling of human language understanding that would be required by a completely intelligent system for teaching advanced learners, (29) one solution is to aim at partial modelling, and to construct language learning materials consisting of interactive dialogue between learner and computer, in which the semantic universe is so drastically restricted that it *is* feasible to expect the system to process all the possible meanings of the words in the lexicon used. This was the solution adopted by Winograd (1972) in his famous SHRDLU program (30), where the universe is limited to a table-top with various geometrical objects on it, which the computer

---

(29) Winograd, T., (1984), "Computer Software for Working with Language", *Scientific American*, 251, 3.
(30) Winograd, T., (1972), *Understanding Natural Language*, Academic Press.

moves around in response to orders given in plain English.

Exercises based on a sublanguage, or restricted domain, of this type are described in Ward (1986). They are designed for helping to develop the linguistic skills of hearing-impaired and language-impaired children. A number of coloured shapes and objects appear, or can be summoned to the screen. The child can move these round, form patterns or discover hidden patterns, but must do this by typing instructions and questions, and by answering questions posed by the system. The child's linguistic competence is expanded by discovering the various language constructs available in the program. In a somewhat similar manner Sampson (1986) describes a system, designed to help children learn to read clocks, which can cope with a wide range of linguistic inputs within a limited semantic area.

Another approach, adopting the same solution of restricting the semantic universe, consists of using the text maze, or adventure game. At each stage in the maze an interaction takes place between learner and system, and the exigencies of the story or scenario are such as to narrow the possibilities down to a point at which the computer can be expected to process any sentence that is at all likely to occur. Labelle describes such a maze in which a simple parser is capable of dealing with any input relevant to the situation (31). A disadvantage, however, of text mazes is that the popularity of adventure games has led to the development of a sort of 'minitelspeak' which has to be discouraged if the scenario is to be useful for language learning. In any case the possibilities of the text maze, in spite of Durrani's spirited advocacy, (32) seem too limited for the advanced learner.

A more promising line to follow is suggested both by Sampson and by Ward, whose shape-manipulating program escapes interestingly from the prevailing tutorial paradigm, a disadvantage of which is, as Sampson points out, the manner in which it "tends to force the learner into a passive role". It may be tempting to fantasise about the ideal CALL system, to imagine a program able to cope, not just with the elementary problems of tense and agreement, but with all those recondite aspects of grammatical and syntactic nicety that, for example, send the advanced learner of literary French ferreting in the utmost recesses of Grevisse, a program that could distinguish and make explicit the difference between *savoir* and *connaître* or between *soupe* and *potage*. Fortunately however, there is no call for such a system. The truth is that the more advanced the learner the less relevant the intrusive tutorial type of CALL is to her/his needs, and the more important it is to get away from the notion of a system that is not only intelligent but all-embracing

(31) Labelle, F., (1986), "Jeux d'Aventure", in Feneuille, J., (Ed) (1986), *Informatique et Enseignement des Langues*, Les Amis de Sèvres, Paris, 122, 2.
(32) See *supra*, Chapter IV.

and all-knowing.

In any case, restricting the semantic universe is only one way of dealing with the problem. It is also only really practicable with near beginners: the learner very rapidly learns how to use the new language, however imperfectly, to manipulate a much wider range of meanings than the computer can, as yet, encompass unaided. Reference is, however, only one aspect of meaning, and, for that matter, there is no law that says that an intelligent system *must* do all the work unaided. The way forward, therefore, would seem to lie in the direction of CALL materials which are semi-intelligent, and which are based on a text rather than on a series of sentences. A semi-intelligent program could be described as a conventional 'dumb' CALL program which employs limited, or not so limited, AI techniques to increase the range of language it can process, give it more power and make it more flexible, but which does not attempt to model the competence of a native speaker. Cook describes a number of such systems (33). In addition to dialogue exercises using the Eliza principle, he describes drills, which the addition of a parser can turn into information-processing exercises, and Cloze exercises which the syntactic parser makes grammatically intelligent.

LITTRE (34) may serve as an example of a semi-intelligent program. It is a translation system, designed to process the literary language used in university prose composition classes and examinations. It does not therefore employ a parser, since it must be able to process input, often very ill-formed, but covering a wide semantic range, in a manner that is sensitive to fairly fine contextual, not to mention stylistic, distinctions and constraints. It does this by checking the learner's input against a database organised on several levels of syntactic analysis. LITTRE can be used as a straight tutorial program, the learner treating the prompts that come from the system as so many questions to answer, or it can be used, more intelligently, as an aid to conjectural or revelatory learning, (35) the learner prodding the system for suggestions, and then deciding on her own which of the various pathways offered she wishes to explore. LITTRE is, however, a 'dumb' system, in that the database must be constructed beforehand on paper, which can be a laborious process if the translation is a difficult one. Typing it into the system is facilitated by an authoring

(33) Cook, V.J. and Fass, D., (1986), "Natural Language Processing by Computer and Language Teaching", *System*, 14, 2, 163-70.
(34) Farrington, B., (1986), "LITTRE, An Expert System For Checking Translation at Sentence Level", in Fox, J., (1986), "Computer Assisted Language Learning", *UEA Papers in Linguistics*, University of East Anglia, Norwich.
(35) Kemmis, S., Atkin, R., Wright, E., (1977) *How do Students Learn?*, Working Papers on Computer-Assisted Learning: UNCAL evaluation studies, *Occasional Publications* 5, Centre for Applied Research in Education, University of East Anglia.

package.

If we remain with the tutorial mode, the best use of the new techniques for advanced learners may well be with the authoring systems, rather than the actual CALL material itself. Sophisticated tutorial materials, such as the ORDI exercises described above, or LITTRE, are time-consuming to construct. Much of the time is spent in analysing and classifying errors made by test batches of learners, selecting or drawing up appropriate explanatory comments and so on. Instead of striving after the chimera of fully automatic processing of either this material or learner input we would do better to try and develop semi-automatic, consultative, systems which would speed up this work of preparation and make it easier, and which would probably improve the finished exercise as well. There is an economic reason also for developing a sophisticated, intelligent, authoring system to construct materials for a relatively simple CALL program. LITTRE is a case in point, since it runs on a micro of which almost any school could afford several examples. It will not matter if its authoring system needs much more expensive hardware than the program itself, since only one such master machine would be needed. This may allay a major misgiving about Intelligent Systems that has not been mentioned so far, namely that their 'ailes de géant' may make them too expensive for any normal school to contemplate purchasing.

What other possibilities are there? CALL of course doesn't *have* to be intelligent, and it certainly doesn't have to be all intelligent. We should beware of the purism of the computer scientist, and his desire to find elegant solutions to intellectual problems, rather than produce materials, exercises, of humdrum everyday usefulness. It may well be that there is still plenty of mileage to be got out of 'dumb' programs, written in that much-despised language BASIC, and running on the most unpretentious of home computers. After all, one of the most interesting innovations of recent years, useful above all for advanced learners, has been Micro-Concord, mentioned above, which can process large quantities of text of any degree of difficulty, and which runs on the smallest home computer available on the British market.

Whichever way is followed, and there are certainly other possibilities that I have not mentioned, or thought of, one thing seems clear. Linguists and the Artificial Intelligentsia must come together and collaborate if progress is to be made. The technology is advancing so fast that it is imperative that we call on each other's expertise if full advantage is to be taken of either. No linguist, or language teacher, or CALL buff is so clever that s/he could not do better with the addition of a little extra intelligence, however Artificial it may seem. On the other hand any Intelligent Tutoring System that ignores or tries to diminish the importance of meaningfulness in language learning is a contradiction in terms.

VII

TOWARDS AN INTELLIGENT SYNTAX CHECKER

J.E. Galletly and C.W. Butcher, with J.Lim How

University of Buckingham

This chapter contains two principal parts : the first aims to present an extremely wide overview of the directions in which we feel Computer Assisted Language Learning should perhaps be moving in the future; and the second, to report on a small project in this field carried out at Buckingham, using PROLOG on an Orion super/minicomputer, and designed to check a small area of French syntax. While it would be temerarious to claim that this project, of a very limited scope, is any sort of real pointer to the future, we do feel that certain of its unconventional aspects may indicate a possibility for new lines of research.

1. The Next Generation: What Future for CALL?

Taking the widest of overviews, it is possible to argue that the processing of natural language by computers, and, with it, CALL, is at present at a crossroads. It is our feeling that the various initiatives within the subject, and the various constraints without, whether in hardware, finance, or public expectations, have reached a 'cusp point'. It will, in our view, either all tend to run out of steam or else begin finally to make a number of major breakthroughs.

On many levels, CALL may be considered to have existed long enough now to have had the chance to acquire a clear *modus vivendi*. Whatever the vicissitudes of funding at the moment, many UK universities have sufficient numbers of semi-dedicated machines, in most cases Acorn BBCs, for normal-sized teaching groups to gain individual hands-on experience. Within the particular field of French, there are several score programs available for use on these machines. A very broad categorisation of them might consist of saying that one major area is demonstration and testing of simple grammatical points within the framework of multiple choice or correct/incorrect question/answer sessions. The other main area is more or less based on games: for instance, anagrams, cloze type exercises, or adventure type situations, where, if the situation itself may be relatively open-ended, the language elements themselves are again comparatively limited.

Programs for language teaching are not, however, limited to language teaching programs. Essay writing may be assisted by use of word processing, with or without spell-checkers, and this often leads to considerable gains in both accuracy and creativity. The teaching of translation, in establishments where this is considered a constructive activity, is greatly enhanced when compared with the model, or rather counter-model, of machine translation. More generally, any activity at all on a computer, whether or not specifically designed for teaching and/or language purposes, may well contribute to language use: for instance constrained or open-ended communication with Minitel services or other machine users; or indeed any activity whatsoever with computers which provides a pretext for discussion in the foreign language concerned.

The potential benefits of all these methods are indisputable. The main one, from the all important view of the student her/himself, is that the (micro-)computer normally provides immediate, individual, uncritical, and unambiguous feedback about some aspect of language performance. Whereas human views on language are often ill informed, evasive, contradictory, or even wrong, the mere fact of being informed by the machine leads the student to believe that error and obscurity are minimised, if only because of the process of formalisation, and s/he is often right.

Nevertheless, we believe that many of the existing initiatives may well prove difficult to sustain. One of the problems is that of the commercial world outside. The educational market represents perhaps 1% of the total national market for hardware and software, and educational software hardly crosses national boundaries at all. The result, then, is that the business world, with which students will increasingly be making comparisons, is apparently in a better position than educational establishments to produce sophisticated and well presented products within a minimal lapse of time. Another problem, in the UK at least, is that of standards. Until now the *ipso facto* standard provided by the BBC machines, at least in language departments, has proved an inestimable advantage for communication, despite the limited memory capacity of these venerable devices. In our view, the future will however be marked by a period of competition between even the Archimedes, with its capacity to operate on PC-DOS, and pure IBM compatible micros.

But the final problem is that of the very methodology, and this, we believe, is where the next few years may well prove crucial. It would seem probable that the degree of complexity of language 'processed' by computers will increase markedly. The evidence from other areas of almost quantum leaps is here indicative. After draughts, where a computer was of world champion level as early as 1959 (1), microcomputers have, after many false starts, reached average club level at chess, can prove theorems in geometry, can do questions from IQ tests. In other words, some element of intelligence has convincingly been demonstrated, often even on the humble micro, and the severest critics have thus been forced to repeatedly reduce the area where 'a mere machine will never be as good as a human being'. Again, from a slightly different angle, expert systems, representing the transcription of human expertise in such subjects as medicine or share dealing, demonstrate behaviour comparable in some respects to that of humans. This remains true even if the methods employed are often the severest of short cuts, with the inevitable consequences of limited areas of competence and of lack of flexibility.

The implications for language are inescapable. Despite the elusiveness of many aspects of the subject, the amount of non-trivial processing of natural language will increase. At the same time, the commercial influence, if only on operating systems or programming languages, will become more and more important. In this perspective, it is impossible to overestimate the importance of word processing. Of course, the computing implementation of present day achievements cannot be considered especially difficult (and one can therefore legitimately ask why, like the walkman, they took so long to be introduced in practical form). But this lack of computing complexity, although it has led many 'pure' computer specialists to dismiss the whole area, probably has little to do with its real potential, which would seem very large indeed. It is our view then that, despite the extra impetus provided by 'desk top publishing', the full effect on many practical areas of even present stages of text processing is still to be felt. Sir Alan Peacock, for instance, has emphasised the extent to which the work of government committees is beginning to be transformed (2); and some language teachers, to bring the subject closer to home, are just beginning to assess the practical and theoretical consequences of this mini-revolution.

As one example, should spelling be taught at all in cases where much of the donkey work can be done by machines? Again, translations and essays, etc., are to be carried out by the student without any external help, goes the unwritten rule, but does this apply to help from a mere computer? The question is especially crucial in those universities where traditional, 3-hour examinations are *not* the only method of evaluation, where, as a consequence, a rich enough student may improve 'take home' work by artificial means. But the problem is not very far away from the examination hall either. Anyone who participated in the incoherent and anguished

---

(1) See Butcher, H.J., (1968), *Human Intelligence: Its Nature and Assessment*, p.133.
(2) In an address at the University of Buckingham, "The Future of Broadcasting", May 1987.

debate about the use of calculators in mathematics and science will understand that the problem of the use of portable language processors is urgent, and should be discussed without delay.

Such, then, was one element of our thinking about a year ago. The huge advantage of word processors and spell-checkers is that they represent real interaction between the user and the computer. Their disadvantage, of course, is that, ultimately, they represent the mere mechanical storing and reproduction of minimal units of language. The word processor itself is even language free (give or take a few diacritics), a fact which demonstrates its conceptual emptiness; and the spell-checker is, in its present avatars, nothing but a word list. The task for the future is thus that of enhancing the substantive but excessively discrete areas of natural language that computers can already cope with. One's awareness, however, of over ambitious projects in all areas of computing, and the often even less justified claims accompanying them, must incite one to a great deal of caution in predicting what can be achieved.

Our next conclusion, therefore, was that the syntax/semantics distinction might prove vital. On the one hand, semantics, with its strong links with philosophy, is a highly contentious area, and contains very few indisputable assertions indeed. The syntax of a given language, in marked contrast, represents a considerable body of accumulated knowledge, in relatively uncontroversial form. Descriptive linguists, who have often replaced the prescriptive ones in recent years, even have an ultimate court of appeal as to the 'correctness' (i.e. existence) of a given 'string' of characters: either submission to competent users of the language in question, or comparison with pre-existing performance in that language. The set of all possible utterances in a language, in other words, is a well defined set; and so is that of utterances which do *not* conform to the language. Ultimately, it may perhaps follow that the distinction between the two sets may be susceptible to rule based treatment; and therefore to treatment by machine based methods. At the same time, syntax is obviously sufficiently broad and deep to present any number of real challenges for the future, in both applied linguistics in general and its subvariety based on computers.

As far as CALL in particular is concerned, studying syntax could thus be a reasonably precise area of research, while at the same time having the interest and prestige of being a subject 'on the cutting edge of human knowledge'. But in fact, at least as important an advantage is that emphasis on 'mere' syntactic processes is of course the substance of much foreign language teaching practice, even where advanced students are concerned. Perhaps as little as half of the feedback process is concerned with what the students 'really' wished to say, or, especially, write; and perhaps as much as half with 'mistakes' on the 'surface' level of spelling, grammar, etc. Many of these errors are in fact on a surprisingly elementary level (3).

Our next piece of heart-searching took us into the more technical area of considering the choice of tools available.

2. *Choice of Programming Language*

Another reason why CALL and, more generally, artificial intelligence applied to languages may be considered at a crossroads is the use of programming language.

BASIC is of course at present the lingua franca in many areas of both CAL and CALL in the United Kingdom. The principal reason is accessibility: the language itself is relatively easy to learn, and easy to use; and it is often included with the micro-computer on sale. Amongst the many dialects, Acorn's BBC-BASIC is universally recognised as being second to none, to such an extent as to have been adopted by at least one notorious arch-rival.

It was of course inevitable that computer purists, or puritans, should decree that more necessarily meant worse, that making the arcane knowledge of the boffins available to the masses was necessarily to adulterate it. The language community, on the other hand, took the eminently sensible view that its interests did not always coincide with those of other users, a view often encapsulated in disdain of 'mere number crunching'. Whatever the underlying reasons, BASIC has in fact proved of inestimable worth to linguists as the standard language, and one can point to such highly creditable achievements within it as Kenney and Kenney's *A Vous la France!* (1986) or Farrington's *Littré* (1987) (4).

The disadvantages of BASIC have also been well rehearsed: in particular, its unstructured nature which, even in the BBC dialect and in not untutored hands, can sometimes lead to unwieldy programs which are difficult to read, and therefore

---

(3) Hares,R. and Elliott, G., (1982), *Compo! French Language Essay Writing.* Designed for both secondary and university level students, *Compo!* reveals how often, in the view of Hares and Elliott, essays are marred by elementary mistakes: the examples quoted (pp. 28 – 30) would seem to be approximately 40% pure spelling, 40% pure agreement problems, and only 20% cases requiring further explanation. The inescapable implication is that, in an overwhelming majority of cases, this formal aspect is an area where computers are likely to be very shortly encroaching on that of students' competence.

(4) Kenney, M-M. and Kenney, M., (1986), *A Vous la France!*, BBC Publications; Farrington, B, *Littré*, 1987 version, Scottish Computer Based French Learning Project, University of Aberdeen.

also difficult to alter without the whole edifice beginning to crumble over one's head. Other disadvantages can be slowness of reaction time, and, as we have seen, limitations of memory in the machines on which it is normally implemented.

Amongst the alternatives we considered, therefore, was Icon, which is a modern derivative of the string processing language SNOBOL. As such it was clearly suited to language processing work. On the other hand, its use is at present largely limited to the United States. Even if work is presently being carried out to 'port' Icon compilers to popular microcomputers available on the British market, we thought it better to play safe, and avoid excessively eccentric choices.

This left as main contenders, amongst those programming languages used by workers in the fields of Artificial Intelligence and Knowledge Engineering, LISP and PROLOG. Both languages are essentially different from BASIC, in that they are very 'high level' ones. In BASIC, a great deal of effort is expended giving detailed instructions to the computer as to how to go about solving the tasks required. LISP and PROLOG, in marked contrast, are 'declarative' languages: they merely state, in duly standardised form, the nature of the task. In this way, the donkey work of specifying the steps for solving the task is delegated to the compiler. The result is much shorter programs, and, hopefully, more elevated and clear sighted programming.

Both languages are, again, suited to string handling; but here this built-in capability exists on many different levels, in a way that models remarkably certain features of natural language. Thus the main structure in both languages is the 'list': a word may be defined as a list of characters; but then a sentence may be defined as a second level list, a list of words; and so on. This sort of recursive possibility is not, however, limited to such definitions. It may be invoked in general even within the procedures, allowing them notably to invoke themselves. The result, as one can imagine, is highly concise and elegant programs.

An excessive degree of elegance may here, however, be dangerous, in the sense that abuse of recurrence leads to potential difficulties. Nevertheless, it is perhaps not entirely too fanciful to imagine that this very danger is indicative of deep parallels between programming and natural languages, as brilliantly demonstrated by Hofstadter (5). In particular, he claims that a) natural language is intrinsically defined by its capacity to cope with the multi-level contradictions produced when one allows formal systems to self-refer by embodying emblematic representations of themselves and that b) this analogy between natural language and computing

---

(5) See Hofstadter, D.R., (1979), *Gödel, Escher, Bach: An Eternal Golden Braid*, New York; Hofstadter, D.R., (1985), *Metamagical Themas*.

languages may be very fruitful indeed for future research in such areas.

Choosing between LISP and PROLOG comes down to a number of possibly ancillary factors. It is not our intention to arbitrate the fierce debate currently going on amongst 'pure' computer scientists as to the intrinsic merits of each. But LISP has the advantage of being more widely available, with more researchers proficient in it, and more existing programs. Against that, it suffers, in our view, from a slightly cumbersome syntax, a proliferation of brackets, which makes programs difficult to read and to adapt.

PROLOG, on the other hand, is a more recent language. It was chosen by the Japanese as the base language for their fifth generation computer projects. This is possibly a sign of its inherent worth; but also a knock-on effect may be produced in the future, and PROLOG may thus become one of the standard languages in artificial intelligence.

More particularly, one can point to two particular advantages of PROLOG. First, it has built-in pattern matching routines, clearly invaluable in the context of repeated searches for given patterns of letters within words, and given words within the text as a whole. Secondly, it has intrinsic modularity. It is therefore especially suitable for not only building prototypes of systems quickly, but also, should this seem useful, adding successive new stages to existing systems (6).

Ultimately the choice of language is determined by its ease and pleasantness of use for a given purpose. (Literary trained scholars may therefore be more convinced by appeal instead to Barthes's 'pleasure of the text', and his insistence on *scriptabilité* ('write-ability') and *lisibilité* ('read-ability').) For us, whatever the reason, it was PROLOG, by half a head.

3. A Brief Introduction to PROLOG

[The aim of this section is to give some of the flavour of the PROLOG programming language, by presenting a few concepts and examples. It is not, however, essential to the understanding of the next section, which describes the project itself in essentially practical terms. Some of the details of the PROLOG implementation itself are, in addition, briefly described after the project.]

---

(6) PROLOG has a very strong compatibility with natural language processing. As just one example, the syntax of some PROLOG compilers has even been extended to enable a particular class of parsers, called 'Definite Clause Grammars', to be written easily (Pereira, C.N., and Warren, D.H.D., (1980) "Definite Clause Grammars for Language Analysis", *Artificial Intelligence*, Vol. 13, p.231.).

Any programming language for AI or expert systems must necessarily have some internal means of representing knowledge. Ideally, a knowledge system will include the following features:

1. a knowledge base, a set of facts and rules;

2. an inference engine, a system to reason with the given facts and rules;

3. an explanation facility, to explain to the user why the system has adopted a particular line of reasoning;

4. user interface, to provide easy-to-use access; and

5. a knowledge acquisition system, a method for acquiring and encoding new knowledge.

In PROLOG, the inference engine is explicitly provided, but great freedom is accorded to the programmer in instituting the others!

The name 'PROLOG' means 'Programming in Logic'. Basically, the programmer's task is to state the problem in terms of defined facts and rules, these rules being expressed as a 'logical' sequence of statements. A PROLOG program, then, comprises a set of known 'facts' (the 'database'), and a set of rules or relations governing the facts, the two together being called the 'knowledge base'. The system solves a problem expressed in terms of a goal by attempting to prove the 'validity' (positive truth value) of this goal on the basis of the given facts and rules. Normally sub-goals will be defined by the system, and then proved separately.

A very simple example may make this much clearer. At a first stage of sophistication, we simply wish to communicate to the system the present indicative conjugation of the verb *avoir*:

> avoir (ai).
> avoir (as).
> avoir (a).
> avoir (avons).
> avoir (avez).
> avoir (ont).

These, then, are PROLOG facts, with *avoir* being called the 'predicate', and *ai*, *as*, etc., the 'argument'.

If we wish to add further information, then we could write the following PRO-LOG facts:

> verb   (avoir, ai).
> verb   (avoir, as).
> .
> .
> .
> verb   (avoir, ont).
> verb   (être, suis).
> verb   (être, es).
> .
> .
> .
> verb   (être, sont).

[Read: 'there exists a verb including parts *avoir* and *ai*',etc.]

Here we have defined a new predicate, called 'verb', and included the infinitive *avoir* or *être* as a second argument to this predicate.

Having given the system a reasonable number of similar facts, like other verb conjugations and tenses, one can then interrogate the system. A question such as

> verb (Inf, sommes).

asks the system to find an Inf (infinitive) such that *sommes* is part of the same verb. (The system does not *know*, of course, that Inf means anything: for it, Inf is just an unknown variable. The capital I on Inf, incidentally, marks it as being a variable rather than a constant (which would begin with a small letter).) The pattern matching facility of PROLOG is then invoked, the database is searched, and the solution

> Inf = être

duly appears on the screen.

Turning now to an example of the *rules*, let us assume that some regular verb stems and verb endings have already been read in, as follows:

reg_stem	(parl).
reg_stem	(port).

.

.

.

reg_stem	(aim).
reg_ending	(e).
reg_ending	(es).

.

.

.

reg_ending   (ent).

If we wish to tell the system now that a verb is in fact made up of a stem plus an ending, we simply write the *rule*:

reg_verb (Stem, Ending):-   reg_stem (Stem),
                            reg_ending (Ending).

[:- is read 'such that', and , is read 'and' (the logical operator).]

A rule, in other words, enables the system to generalise, to cope, in the present example, with *any* regular verb. More generally, a rule is always of the form

Head:- Body.

where Head is what is being defined, and Body is what is already known, being comprised of a predicate or predicates.

The power of PROLOG is of course that this process may be repeated as many times as one wishes, so as to build up knowledge bases of indefinite complexity. But even within the simple database of verb conjugations, one *can* imagine non-trivial problems which could be quickly solved. Assuming that 'all' French conjugations have been read in, one could then ask which verbs have an identical present and *passé simple*. Ask the average human user, and you might receive the response '*dit*'.

Let us assume that the facts have been entered, for all verbs, in the form:

.
.
.

verb (present, dit).

.

.

.

verb (passé-simple, dit).

.

.

.

and that a general rule has been indicated, of the form:

find (Tense1, Tense2, Part):- verb (Tense1, Part),
                               verb (Tense2, Part),
                               Tense1 \ = Tense2.

(where \ = is the inequality operator).

Then a query of the form:

find (present, passé-simple, X).

would elicit the response:

$$X = dit$$

But then as many further instances as wished may be obtained by repeatedly typing a semi-colon (;), which will give

$$X = finit$$
$$X = choisit, \text{ etc.}$$

Again, to enquire which *different* verbs have an identical part, and assuming that the facts have been entered in the form:

.

.

.

verb (past-subjunctive, crusse, croître).

.

.

.

verb (past-subjunctive, crusse, croire).

.

.

.

together with a rule:

find (Inf1, Inf2) :- verb (Tense, Part, Inf1),
                      verb (Tense, Part, Inf2),
                      Inf1 \ = Inf2.

Then a query of the form:

find (A, B).

will elicit the response:

B = croire
A = croître

In sum, PROLOG is a highly flexible and elegant language, one which is perfectly adapted, we believe, to processing natural language.

4. The Project

The project was a final year undergraduate Computer Science one undertaken by J. Lim How, and supervised by J. Galletly (School of Sciences) and W. Butcher (School of Humanities).

It was principally a pilot study into the development of tools for computer assisted teaching of French language at the University of Buckingham. Besides students taking French to degree level, Buckingham has numerous students taking French as a supporting course from beginner's to post A-level standard. The project was not intended however to be a *pure* CALL project, for two reasons: 1. students are not especially orientated towards the theory or practice of teaching; and 2. it was thought that the results of the project would be of more interest if the system exhibited some aspects of the general, open-ended use of language characteristic of human communication, rather than simply leading the user through a predefined and closed teaching situation. In other words, the system should demonstrate some small degree of machine intelligence or expert knowledge. For the reasons explained above, it was considered that the specific area of French syntax was sufficiently wide as to allow a large number of interesting possibilities.

5. General Requirements of a CALL System

We list below some important general features which we believe any CALL system should possess. The list is not exhaustive nor original. Barchan *et al.* (7), for example, have expressed similar views: 1. the system should have some pedagogic value and provide an interesting environment in which to learn; 2. the system should provide quasi-immediate responses, users should not be kept waiting unduly for system responses; 3. the error reporting should be helpful to the user, the messages should be meaningful; 4. the system should correct user errors wherever possible; 5. the system should accept *free* input, the system should be wide ranging enough to cope with arbitary sentences and not confine the user to a narrow range of input; 6. the system should be robust, user errors or unexpected answers should not make the system crash; 7. the system should be capable of expansion, new ideas, new approaches, new areas should be readily accommodated; 8. consequently, it must not be idiosyncratic: it must use methods that are both transparent and reproducible.

In the following sections, we provide a mainly practical and linguistic description of the project.

6. Area of Investigation

The human method of constructing sentences in a foreign language, at least at the elementary and intermediate level, includes applying, implicitly or explicitly, certain rules of grammar. It is this notion which we decided to use: instead of following the traditional approach of parsing, we based the 'syntax checker' on various heuristics about French grammar in certain selected domains. These heuristics or rules form the 'knowledge base' of our system, with rules being applied to a French sentence to see if the sentence conforms to them or not. Our method, then, is slightly reductionist, but no more so than many accounts in textbooks.

Two closely related areas of French syntax which seemed compact enough for

---

(7) Barchan, J., Woodmansee, B., and Yazdani, M., (1986), "A PROLOG Based Tool For French Grammar Analysis", *Instructional Science*, vol. 14, pp.21 – 48.

this project suggested themselves. These are

negation

and

object pronoun order in verbal phrases.

Both areas are regular enough to allow some sort of systematic treatment and are also sufficiently different from their parallels in English to offer interest to non-native speakers of French. Barchan *et al.* (1986) have pointed out research evidence for the necessity of putting bounds on the learning area, only specific points of grammar should be dealt with.

Negation

Negation has the advantage that the nine main operative words

ne ... pas, point, jamais, rien, plus, personne, nullement, guere

are morphologically invariant, with the exception of *n'* being a variant of *ne*. On the other hand, there are major disadvantages. Although normally *ne* and one of *pas, point, jamais*, etc., must *both* be present in the sentence, there are certain exceptions. These include *ne* on its own, *pas, point*, etc., on their own, and cases involving *ne* and *ni* in combination. There is also the situation where these words are used as nouns or other parts of speech, for more than half of them, *pas, point, rien, plus, personne*, are not necessarily negation words at all. In the event, due to time constraints, we adopted the practical expedient of bypassing these problems, and requesting the user not to be so perverse as to introduce such sentences as *un plus n'est plus plus qu'un rien!*

The basic rules implemented in the program are as follows:

1. *ne* can be followed (but not immediately) by any negation word in a sentence. There has to be at least one word (including a verb) in between. For example, *Je n'entends personne* ('I hear nobody') is accepted, but *Je ne personne* is rejected.

2. *pas* and *point* in the same sentence are considered ungrammatical, as is a combination of *pas* or *point* with *jamais, rien, plus, personne, nullement* and/or *guere*. But a combination of two or more of this last list *is* allowed, provided that the same negation word does not appear twice in the sentence. e.g. *Je n'ai pas point vu Paul*

is rejected, but *Je n'ai jamais rien vu de pareil* ('I have never seen anything like it') is accepted. On the other hand, as explained above, 'perverse' sentences like *Rien n'est plus beau que rien* are technically correct but are treated as errors.

3. *rien* and *personne* are the only negation words which can precede *ne* but in that case they must do so immediately. e.g. *Rien ne va plus!* ('No more bets please!') is accepted, but *Rien va ne plus* is rejected.

While these few rules are of course far from a complete description of negation in French, they were found in practice to be sufficient to 'trap' many learner errors.

Object Pronoun Order

Verbs and their preceding pronouns, with optional negation, present a complex but well formed structure in French, and one which conveniently supplements the above.

Sequences of up to eight words can be dealt with by the system, which can thus on occasion seem quite impressive. At the same time, seven of the words are from very well defined categories, and there is little possibility of intervening words: two advantages making the implementation much easier.

The various combinations possible are summarised in the following table, which covers all indicative tenses, together with negative imperatives:

ne	me	le	lui	y	en	*VERB*	pas
	te	la	leur				point
	se	les					jamais
	nous						rien
	vous						plus
							personne
							nullement
							guère

Of course, almost any or all of these words could be absent. The only necessary element in the sequence is in fact the verb. Accordingly, our analysis of pronoun order starts by trying to identify the verb in the sentence entered and, only when this has been successfully carried out, examining the pronoun order.

This identification is a major problem. Various lines of attack might have been possible here, including checking words against an existing dictionary, looking at the context of words in their surroundings and examining the endings of words. The first approach was used by Barchan *et al.*: trailing characters are stripped off a word until a morphological root is recognised in the dictionary. But the word-ending approach looked the most interesting to us: the program would attempt to locate a verb in a sentence by examining the endings of all the words. In the event, we adopted the opposite method to Barchan's, stripping off *leading* characters until a recognisable *ending* appeared. Given that the longest endings were thus searched for first, this had the advantage of identifying -*tes* as distinct from -*es*, as distinct from -*s*.

Another problem is that, in some tenses, French verbs are in two main parts: the auxiliary *avoir*/*être* plus the past participle. Also other words, such as *même* or *indubitablement* may intervene before the participle. The solution adopted was to consider the finite part of the verb as the operative part and to ignore the participles. This decision is in line with speakers' subjective impressions that the auxiliary is the vital part, and it also obviates the problem of agreement of the past participle (8).

As a first step, some highly simplistic rules for identifying verbs by their endings were identified. We adopted the practical expedient of accepting the affirmative, negative and imperative forms of the verbal phrase, but not interrogatives. (Infinitives may, of course, be present but are in any case ignored by the program, which simply identifies the finite verb.)

The basic French verb endings may be summarised as follows:

1. words with endings -*it*, -*ai*, -*as*, -*ez*, -*ais*, -*ait*, -*ent*, -*est*, -*ons*, -*ont*, -*iens*, -*ient*, are *probably* verbs

and

2. words with endings -*a*, -*e*, -*s*, -*es*, -*is*, -*tes* are *possibly* verbs.

It was decided, however, that these rules were of limited usefulness on their own: many words which are not verbs have endings in -*e*, -*s*, -*es*, etc. Also, the distinction possibly/probably would be very difficult to implement in practical terms. As one way of alleviating the problem, the program was given some more information:

---

(8) Or past participles, as in the various forms of *surcomposé*, e.g. *il a eu fait*.

1. a small dictionary containing some common non-verbs with the above endings is searched before the verb rules are applied. A successful matching is then ignored as a verb;

2. a dictionary containing the complete conjugation of three of the most common irregular verbs, *avoir, être, aller*, is also searched before the verb rules are applied. A word matching with a dictionary entry is taken to be a verb.

If the use of these two dictionaries does not work, the situation clearly becomes more problematic. For example, there is the homonym problem: *porte* is possibly a verb, *le porte* certainly is, *la porte* just possibly is, *je la porte* certainly is, and so on.

In the event, we recognised that there is limited knowledge in the system and, due to time constraints, instead of trying to identify the verb via further rules and facts based, for instance, on the immediate grammatical context, resorted to user interaction. Of course appealing to the human user reduces the autonomy of the program. It does, nevertheless, increase the user's involvement, which may be an important consideration in an educational context. In these 'awkward' cases, we have to assume that the user has some minimal knowledge of French syntax, i.e. can identify whether a given word is a verb or not.

At this point, a major methodological problem became apparent. A given sentence must, for our purposes, contain a verb, but it may contain, in fact, any number of different verbs, and thus it is hard to know when to stop looking for them. The solution adopted was to assess each word in the sentence in order, and not to attempt to define a 'main' verb. Some examples may make the different cases clearer:

J'ai déjà donné ('I have already made a contribution')

Nous allons gagner la Coupe ('We are going to win the Cup')

Vivre est souffrir ('To live is to suffer')

La musique adoucit les moeurs ('Music makes for gentler manners')

The first three are accepted as such, since the program recognises *ai*, *allons*, and *est* as definite verbs. In cases like *adoucit*, however, the program announces to the user that the word is possibly a verb, and ask her/him to confirm it. In other words, by means of progressively less elegant and autonomous, but more complete methods, a verb is always identified. In theory, there are no situations where the machine simply 'gives up'.

The analysis of the pronouns proved considerably easier to implement. Use of PROLOG means that the system can identify with relative facility the two negation words and the various combinations of up to five pronouns. It can then check whether the canonical order is respected. It finally either notifies the user of any errors detected in the order of the words, or confirms that it has not detected any errors of this sort. Thus

N'y va pas ('Don't go there')

Il n'y en avait plus ('There weren't any left') and

Je le lui donnai ('I gave it to him')
are accepted.

Contrariwise,

Je lui le donnai

J'ai lui donne
are not accepted (9).

To sum up, then, what happens in terms of screen presentation: once a prompt mark appears on the screen, the user can enter a French sentence. In certain cases, he will be asked, successively, if certain words are verbs or not. Finally, the machine issues a verdict as to its assessment of grammaticality (covering both the verb(s) and the other appropriate elements of the sentence). It finally produces a prompt, inviting the user to enter another sentence.

7. Further Details of Implementation

PROLOG is ideal for expressing the heuristics and dictionaries which form the intelligence of this system.

The dictionaries are written as PROLOG facts, e.g. the individual negation

---

(9) It may be noted that the system does not pronounce on whether a given combination makes sense. But this, in our view, is perfectly sensible. Cases like *Je le lui en donne* or even *Je ne le lui y en ai pas donné* are at least perverse. The reason why native or other competent speakers hesitate is doubt as to what nouns all the pronouns could refer to. The problem is ultimately therefore on the semantic rather than the syntactic level, and would thus seem counter productive for treatment by computer based methods at the present moment.

words are written as:

negation   (ne).
negation   (pas).

.

.

.

negation   (guère).

When a sentence is read in by the program, individual characters are combined to form words and the words are stored in a PROLOG list structure. Each word in the sentence is then inspected in turn using PROLOG's pattern matching facility to access the dictionary until a word is recognised.

1. In the negation part, if a negation word is found, then the predefined negation rules are invoked, to examine each of the remaining words in the sentence to see if the sentence conforms or not.

2. In the object pronoun part, each word in the sentence is checked to see whether it is one of the three irregular verbs. Otherwise leading characters are stripped off the word one at a time and the resultant 'stub' compared with the verb endings in the facts database. If a verb ending is recognised, then the user is prompted that the word is either probably or possibly a verb. Once a verb has been asserted, then the object pronoun rules are invoked to analyse the preceding words so as to check that any object pronouns before the verb are both correctly formed and correctly placed. Finally, either correction or congratulation messages are shown on screen.

8. Conclusion

This final year student project posed real and interesting problems; it also generated a great deal of cooperation between the departments involved, and even produced interest from other members of the University.

It was deliberately pitched at a relatively high level, since marketing the result was not an aim and it was felt that the project might as well therefore tackle some substantive area of French grammar. As such, it clearly required a highly heuristic approach, one that may even seem to some people non-conventional, in contrast with, for instance, approaches based on parsing. Also, some of the obstacles encountered could not entirely be removed within the time available, but had to be detoured around. Nevertheless, the fundamental aim was certainly met: that of constructing a program which could accept a very wide range of input, and could analyse it in terms of certain well defined grammatical constraints. Without resorting to the brute force method of storing a large bank of predefined questions and answers, a 'semi-intelligent' response is effectively obtained. More precisely, the program provides the user with very quick, appropriate, and reasonably accurate information in an interactive fashion, and this must surely be considered an achievement in the notoriously slippery world of natural language.

This is not to say that the project does not have room for further improvement and extension. It would be very useful, obviously, if sentences containing more than one negative structure could be read in, like *je ne marche plus et je ne cours jamais*. More generally, it is conceivable to use fuzzy logic to deal with cases of 'possibly/probably a verb' in a less cut-and-dried fashion. This would have the additional advantage of being closer to what humans actually do when presented with an ambiguous structure like *sanctionner* or *je suis*: they seem normally to suspend final judgement, and seek further information in the subsequent words, before 'backtracking' to the source of ambiguity.

In fact, certain cases of lexical ambiguity, if on a simple level, may be a fruitful area for further computer based work. Cases quoted earlier, like *porte* vs *le porte*, etc., are extremely context based; and, even for human users, often in practice pass through a stage of hesitation, involving something like fuzzy logic. It would, nevertheless, be relatively easy for a given pair of homonyms, such as *porte-porte*, *pas-pas* or even *manoeuvre* (m.) – *manoeuvre* (f.), to undergo a process of 'disambiguisation' by means of certain key context pointers. Indeed, this is the most obvious failing, and perhaps the easiest remedied, of the current generation of spell-checkers: their limitation to single word analysis. The word itself for this, 'syntax checker', has unfortunately been trivialised by American programs that do little more than check for odd brackets or typing errors like *the the*. Perhaps the next stage forward, for both CALL and the business world, is programs carrying out semi-intelligent analyses of language: real syntax checkers dealing with real linguistic problems.

We will be the first to buy!

VIII

LANGUAGE TUTORING WITH PROLOG

Masoud Yazdani

University of Exeter

1. Introduction

The best way to learn a foreign language is to spend time with native speakers of that language interacting meaningfully with them, but this is impractical for many and too costly. Many other approaches to second language teaching have been tried, each with differing degrees of success. The most recent have used language laboratories and computer-based instruction. There are shortcomings inherent in these systems: the teaching medium (audio tapes, computer programs) only knows just as much as it has been told, and has no 'knowledge' of its own, which it can draw on and use to respond to developments.

Our research aims to utilise Artificial Intelligence (AI) techniques to aid the learning of human languages. In its embryonic form it consists of a suite of programs which analyse users' sentences in a chosen language and offer advice on grammatical errors (1). These systems have some knowledge of the language they are attempting to teach and know about the common misconceptions of novice language learners. More recently we have developed a general-purpose *shell* called LINGER which, when supplied with the databases specific to a language, will teach the grammar of that language. The motivation behind this work lies in the duplication of effort and code involved in the separate development of tutoring systems for languages which show so many common features.

The idea of using a *shell* is common currency in commercial applications of AI known as Expert Systems. Many AI vendors sell general-purpose *shells* which can then be supplied with rules specific to a domain and turned into fully functioning systems for legal, tax and other forms of advice giving. While in theory such shells offer the computational power to deal with applications in a variety of diverse domains, in principle each shell is most suitable for a closely related set of

---

(1) Barchan, J., Woodmansee, B.J. and Yazdani, M., (1986), "A PROLOG-based Tool for French Grammar Analysis", *Instructional Science*, Vol.14, pp.21 – 48.

applications. The idea of using an Intelligent Tutoring shell has also found support for educational applications of AI. As described by Sleeman (2), a shell is 'a system which is datadriven, and so can cope with different domains; specific knowledge of the domain is contained in the domain database'. Sleeman's shell called PIXIE, attempts remediation for students performing arithmetic operations. It would be too much to hope that a shell developed for arithmetic would be suitable for such a different application as language teaching. However, it seems fruitful to look at the potential of developing LINGER as a counterpart to systems such as PIXIE.

By using an AI approach we think it is possible to build computing systems which have a basic knowledge of the subject matter they are teaching and which can learn from their own experience. This means that there is no restriction on which sentences are used by the learner for practising her/his new language. The user can type any sentence s/he wishes and our current systems attempt to deal with this. Obviously we are far from the ideal situation and that is why this has become a research project!

The project has confronted us with a large number of questions requiring further research. An examination of these questions may help others to tackle the problem. Firstly, the critical question is whether we should build on the general purposeness of the shell or should we build more 'tailor made' systems? Which approach would be more satisfactory from a student's point of view? Secondly, is it in fact feasible for a teacher with a limited knowledge of computer programming to produce a system for a new language using the shell? Thirdly, our systems while strong on the knowledge of how to do grammar analysis, are weak on the representation of 'teaching skills' appropriate to language teaching. How could we encode these skills into our systems?

In addition, as we start to test our systems with potential users, we shall need to address the broader pedagogical issues in the use of this new technology.

In this chapter we aim to introduce interested readers to the basic principles behind our work and the architecture of our systems. As our systems are programmed in PROLOG (3) we shall use this language for the purpose of exposition. The reader need not be familiar with the language in order to follow the chapter. We shall point out the features of the language which implicitly form part of the

(2) Sleeman, D., (1987), "PIXIE : A Shell for Developing Intelligent Tutoring Systems" in Lawler and Yazdani (eds.), *Artificial Intelligence and Education*, Vol.1, Ablex Publishing, Norwood, New Jersey, pp.239 – 265.

(3) Bratko, I., (1986), *Prolog Programming for Articifial Intelligence*, Addison Wesley Publishing, Reading, Ma.

design of our systems. If a more primitive programming language was to be used most of the facilities offered by PROLOG would need to be incorporated as a part of the system itself.

PROLOG was first chosen as it was most suitable for natural language processing tasks. However, the use of PROLOG as a tool has shaped our view of how one should build tutoring systems. PROLOG is a declarative language, where the programmer keeps the definition of *what* is to be done separate from *how* it is to be done. This distinction has enabled us to offer an architecture which would allow teachers to specify *what* they would like done and for us to worry about finding *how* to get the task done. We shall point out the views derived from our use of PROLOG and compare the architecture of our systems to other proposals.

2. Syntactic Structures

The appreciation that human languages such as English have a reasonably clear structure is attributed to Chomsky (4) who has proposed that this structure can be captured by the use of a set of rewrite rules.

The idea is that sentences: 'Steve liked the fish' and 'John boiled the eggs' have a similar structure independent of their meaning. Moreover 'Mary kissed the Moon' could, perhaps, be considered to have the same syntactic structure but would be deemed either meaningless or very weird by most people. Significantly, Chomsky argued that these three sentences had the same syntactic structure.

Obviously we need to distinguish between the words of the language such as eggs, fish, etc. and the syntactic classes such as subject, noun, etc. A grammar of the kind Chomsky used, with major simplification, is as follows:

$$
\begin{array}{lcl}
\text{NP} & \longrightarrow & \text{DET + NOUN} \\
\text{NP} & \longrightarrow & \text{NAME} \\
\text{VP} & \longrightarrow & \text{VERB + NP} \\
\text{VP} & \longrightarrow & \text{VERB} \\
\text{DET} & \longrightarrow & \text{[the]} \\
\text{VERB} & \longrightarrow & \text{[liked, boiled, kissed]} \\
\text{NOUN} & \longrightarrow & \text{[fish, eggs, Moon]} \\
\text{NAME} & \longrightarrow & \text{[Steve, John, Mary]}
\end{array}
$$

Using the above grammar we can see that all three sentences have the following structure:

---

(4) Chomsky, N., (1956), *Syntactic Structures*, Mouton, The Hague.

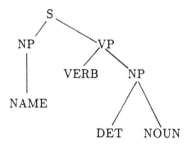

The grammar presented here is considerably more simple than that originally suggested by Chomsky, or that currently used by Chomskian linguists. Further, some new schools of linguistics doubt Chomsky's view of the grammar. Nevertheless let us assume that someone could supply us with a grammar for English. Could we then write a program which would check if a sentence uttered by a speaker is syntactically correct? This may, to some people, appear as a futile exercise. They would argue that as long as the hearer understands what the speaker means, it does not really matter if what was uttered was syntactically correct or not. Although there is some truth in this view, there is also some truth in the view that syntactically correct sentences are easier to understand than a word pot pourri.

Making a meaningful utterance depends very much upon correct syntactic structure, and it is this that we shall deal with here.

Firstly, to write a Prolog program which could check if 'Steve liked the fish' is correct, we need to write the grammar in a form that is understandable to Prolog. For this we shall use a predicate called 'rewrite' in place of $\longrightarrow$ and another called 'followed-by' in place of +. Therefore the statement 'rewrite S by NP followed by VP' would correspond to the first rule of the grammar:

```
10    rewrite(sentence, followed-by(np,vp)).
11    rewrite(np,followed-by(det, noun)).
12    rewrite(np,name).
13    rewrite(vp,followed-by(verb,np)).
14    rewrite(vp,verb).
```

For the moment we have a simple dictionary of known facts

```
20    known([the],det).
```

```
21    known([fish],noun).
22    known([steve],name).
23    known([liked],verb).
```

The following set of 3 Prolog rules would be a satisfactory way of recognising a sentence

```
1.0   is-a(LIST,CATEGORY):-
1.1                         rewrite(CATEGORY,X),
1.2                         is-a(LIST,X).
2.0   is-a(LIST,X):-
2.1                         known(LIST,X).
3.0   is-a(LIST,followed-by(A,B)):-
3.1                         cat(X,Y,LIST),
3.2                         is-a(X,A),
3.3                         is-a(Y,B).
```

The first version of 'is-a' is rather straightforward. It states that if the grammar has a rule which translates the category we are after to another (such as NP $\longrightarrow$ NAME), try 'is-a' again with that category.

The second version of 'is-a' deals with the situation when LIST is broken down to an individual element which we might know as part of our dictionary.

The third version deals with cases in the grammar when a category is broken into two, such as

S $\longrightarrow$ NP + VP.

In this case we need to find two parts X and Y to our LIST where X can be proven to be the category on the left of + and Y to be proven to be the category to the right of +.

Further, for the moment let us not involve ourselves with the issues of inputting the sentences neatly, and assume that the sentence is presented in the form of a list of its constituent words:

[steve,liked,the,fish]

All we need to do now is to make a query to our database of the form

?- is-a([steve,liked,the,fish],sentence).

This would result in Prolog searching for a definition of 'is-a' and settling for the first one it finds. Therefore we now have through line 1.0.

LIST = [steve,liked,the,fish]   and   CATEGORY = sentence

Then 1.1 would look for rewrite(sentence,X) taking us to 10 which would result in

X = followed-by(np,vp)

After this, 1.2 would result in another look for is-a ([steve,liked,the, fish], followed-by(np,vp)). This would only succeed in 3.0 resulting

LIST = [steve,liked,the,fish]
A = np
B = vp

3.1 would look for the easiest way of finding an X and Y which, when concatenated, would make [steve,liked,the,fish] and would come up with

X = [steve]
Y = [liked,the,fish]

3.2 then would look for is-a [steve],np) which takes us back to new is-a of the form 1.0.

LIST = steve
CATEGORY = np

1.1 rewrite(np,X) would use 12 and come up with X=name. 3.2 would then look for is-a([steve],name). This would result in another look at 1.0 and 1.1 trying to rewrite(name,X). This would fail, however, as there is no rewrite rule for the category name in the database. We now go back (or in PROLOG jargon 'backtrack') to our choice of 'is-a' definition to 2.0 and in 2.1 checking for known([steve],name), which would succeed.

We can now attempt

is-a([liked,the,fish],vp)

As an exercise we leave it to the reader to work out how the Prolog would go about proving that [liked,the,fish] is a verb phrase.

3. A Simple Tutoring System

Let us now assume that a newcomer to the English language offers the following to our system

[the, steve, liked, the, fish]

Our system is obviously going to spend a great deal of effort working on it before saying 'no', meaning that it is not a sentence. One way to improve on this is to add a new rule to our database

```
known(X,noun):-
      known(X,name),
      write('names of people such as'),
      write(X),
      write('do not need a determiner').
```

In this way the not-so-perfect sentence is recognised with a message also being printed, which could be a way of using our system for educational purposes. This representation of 'deviation from the norm' would also make our system less dependent on a rigid grammar where we hypothesise deviations from our expectation and signal our interpretation to the user.

One major factor in the success of systems such as ours is a good taxonomy of the popular mistakes novice speakers make and the most effective way of providing remedial advice.

Sleeman (5) has proposed that the computer itself could be used a tool for collecting such 'mal-rules'. In contrast we have relied on the knowledge of human teachers to find and add such information to the system in an incremental fashion. Error collection and analysis may well be a promising by-product of this work.

(5) Sleeman, D., (1987), 'PIXIE : A Shell for Developing Intelligent Tutoring Systems', art.cit.

LINGER (6) is a more complex system in its architecture and scope than the simple example given here. However, LINGER's knowledge is distributed in very much the same proportions on these four levels. The user of LINGER need not know about PROLOG or computer programming in order to use it. The task of the user is to provide databases consisting of the grammar, dictionary and bug catalogue of the language in a clearly specified format. In fact, the task is simplified by the existence of demonstration databases for French, German, Italian and Spanish. The user would then modify the appropriate database to make it fit her/his teaching needs.

4. The Basic Architecture

We subscribe to the four part model of Anderson and colleagues for a tutoring system (7): that the system must be capable of rich interaction with the tutees, know how to teach, and who and what it is teaching. These are the four architectural components which justify the use of 'intelligent' in this particular context. Anderson calls these Student-Tutor Interface, Tutoring Knowledge, Bug Catalogue and the Ideal Student Model.

Our own model of the components of an Intelligent Tutoring System is shown in the following table. We differ from Anderson in that for each of the four components we have listed two attributes. The left-hand side column consists of the sources of knowledge while the right-hand side shows the procedures necessary to put that knowledge to use.

Components of an Intelligent Tutoring Systems

1. Domain Knowledge	+	Inference Engine
2. Bug Catalogue	+	User Modeler
3. Tutoring Skills	+	Planner
4. Explanation Patterns	+	Student Tutor Interface

The domain knowledge in the simple tutoring system of the previous section was the grammar rewrite rules and the dictionary of known facts. The inference engine was provided by the PROLOG system as an inbuilt facility. In our system a simple 'is-a' managed to direct the inference engine to deliver the goods. The bug catalogue in

(6) See Barchan, J., (1987), "Language Independent Grammatical Error Reporter", M.Phil. Thesis, University of Exeter.

(7) Anderson, J.R., Boyle, C.F. and Reiser, B.J., (1985), "Intelligent Tutoring Systems", *Science*, Vol. 228, pp.456 – 462.

the example consisted of the single rule about the superfluous 'the'. We did not in fact do much with the discovery of the error as far as building a model of the user is concerned. The two further levels of tutoring skills and explanation were also missing in any significant form from the system. The explanation offered consisted of a canned text 'the names of people like X do not need a determiner' and for planning the tutoring task we did even less!

The fact that our systems are short of knowledge in some levels is not to say that we feel they are unnecessary but that one needs to start from somewhere. We chose to start from the domain knowledge level as it was the area in which more documented material existed from the discipline of linguistics. Nevertheless our current work aims at addressing the other levels. We feel most other workers who plan to work on building tutoring systems need to ask themselves some of the questions regarding the architecture of their systems that we have done. Some relevant questions are presented in the following table.

Questions regarding the Architecture of a Tutoring System?

Does the software know the subject it is proposing to teach?
Has the software an open architecture?
Can it be extended by the teacher?
Is the software capable of user modelling?
Can the software offer individualised instruction?
Can the software learn new knowledge by interacting with the student?

Issues relating to these questions are studied in more detail elsewhere (8) where we also look at another set of questions related to the environment within which the final system is used. The LOGO community of research workers (9) have shown that their system without itself being 'intelligent' can lead to exceptional educational insights. The fact that people seem to learn even without formal instruction seems to support their conviction.

In our work we have attempted to find an approach which is based on the principle of incorporating 'knowledge' inside our systems as well as leaving room for the students to explore well beyond the architectural potential of the systems. It

---

(8) Yazdani, M., (1987), "Articifial Intelligence for Tutoring", in Whiting and Bell (eds.), *Tutoring and Monitoring Facilities for European Open Learning*, North Holland, pp.239 –248.

(9) Papert, S., (1980), *Mindstorms, Children, Computers and Powerful Ideas*, Basic Books, New York.

is for this reason that we feel other researchers should also take note of this second set of questions along with the first.

Questions regarding the Environment of a Tutoring System

Does it allow the student to explore alternatives, or does it force her/him to follow a pre-set route?

How much time is the user expected to spend with the computer?

How much 'off-computer activity is generated by the system?'

How does it encourage off-computing activity?

Does it encourage joint project work (2/3 users using the system together)?

A good example of a system which has scored high on both set of questions above, is SOPHIE (10). SOPHIE achieves this by supplementing computer system for teaching electronic trouble shooting with a four part training course exploiting game playing and other ideas beyond the capabilities of the system. For example, the students spend some time playing against one another, diagnosing each other's chosen faults on the system.

5. Future Plans

We are aware of many shortcomings in our current systems and are currently proposing to start a new project which goes beyond LINGER. We believe that languages are learned and not taught, and we intend to build an environment around our systems within which the novices are motivated to learn through their own initiative. The context of the our project is the international electronic mail. We intend to encourage language learners to communicate with their pen pals electronically. The difference here is that the intended mail message will first be subjected to one of our language analysers. The user will be helped to correct her/his message to an adequate level of grammatical correctness. Furthermore, our system will make sure that no words or grammatical constructs from the mother tongue are carried over to the message in the new language. The message will then be transmitted to a human pen pal who would reply either in the same language or the mother tongue of the first person, which would probably be the second language of the second user.

Beyond the correction of syntactic errors we hope that our new system could

(10) See Brown, J.S., Burton, R.R. and de Kleer, J., (1982), "Pedagogical, natural language and knowledge engineering techniques in SOPHIE I, II and III", in Sleeman, D. and Brown, J.S. (eds.), (1982), *Intelligent Tutoring Systems*, Academic Press, pp.227 – 282.

build a model of the user's knowledge and misconceptions about the language s/he is learning. We plan to do this by providing the new generation of our systems with two grammars, one of the mother tongue and the other of the target language. By this means we could see the way in which the structure of the person's native grammar interferes with the performance in the new language.

We anticipate that using our system for example, an Italian could communicate with an English pen friend, each learning the language of the other in the process of discussing topics of mutual interest. A by-product of this interaction would be a record of the computer's hypothesis about the reasons behind user's mistakes. We hope that we could start looking at the issues involved in automatic machine learning. Machine learning has a major role to play in the future development of any AI system (11). Any good teacher is learning about the pupils and the subject matter as s/he carries out the task. Computer based systems ideally should not be exempt from this important part of good teaching behaviour. Using machine learning techniques we hope to infer the grammar which would account for a user's sentences in each mail message. We hope that this knowledge 'learnt' while the user is using the system could be used to make the system more adaptable.

Our systems would obviously not be capable of dealing with the semantics of the messages and the users would need to ask for clarification if the meaning of any message was not clear. We hope that in the long term we could also deal with the issue of semantics by introducing an AI pen pal at the other end. For the moment, however, our feet are firmly on the ground! (12)

(11) Partridge, D., (1986), *AI : Applications in the future of Software Engineers*, Ellis Horwood, Chichester
(12) Our work has been supported by two studentships from SERC and grants from ESRC and the MSC. I am grateful to my colleagues Paul O'Brien, Keith Cameron, Jo Uren and Judith Wusteman for their continuous support.